MIRBEAU'S FICTIONS
FM15

Copyright © Christopher Lloyd 1996

The right of Christopher Lloyd to be identified as the author of this work has been asserted by him in accordance with the Copyright, Designs and Patents Act 1988.

Published by Manchester University Press
Oxford Road, Manchester M13 9NR, UK
and Room 400, 175 Fifth Avenue, New York, NY 10010, USA
www.manchesteruniversitypress.co.uk

Distributed exclusively in the USA by
Palgrave, 175 Fifth Avenue, New York NY 10010, USA

Distributed exclusively in Canada by
UBC Press, University of British Columbia, 2029 West Mall,
Vancouver, BC, Canada V6T 1Z2

British Library Cataloguing-in-Publication Data
A catalogue record for this book is available from the British Library

Library of Congress Cataloging-in-Publication Data
A catalog record for this book is available from the Library of Congress

ISBN 978 0 7190 8590 1 *paperback*

First published 1996 by Durham Modern Languages Series

This edition first published 2011 by Manchester University Press

Printed by Lightning Source

Mirbeau's Fictions

Christopher Lloyd

Durham Modern Languages Series

UNIVERSITY OF DURHAM 1996

CONTENTS

	Preface	vii
1.	The Quest for Mirbeau	1
2.	Humour, Cruelty, Caricature	17
3.	Petals of Blood	33
4.	In My Lady's Chamber	52
5.	Mirbeau's Hedgehog	68
6.	Travelling Man	87
	Conclusion	104
	Bibliography	106

Preface

Though his name may mean little to readers in the United Kingdom, in his own country Octave Marie Henry Mirbeau (1848–1917) is neither an obscure nor a forgotten figure. At the height of his career, he was at once a well-paid journalist, a successful novelist and playwright, a social campaigner and a foresighted art collector. And today, many of his books are still readily available in the major paperback collections of French publishers. His best plays remain in the theatrical repertory (witness a long-running revival of *Les Affaires sont les affaires* in 1994–95), while his novels and stories have also inspired posthumous theatrical adaptations; moreover, his engaging satirical perception of the hypocrisies and grotesqueries of the Belle Epoque stimulated directors as diverse as Jean Renoir and Luis Buñuel to turn the novel *Le Journal d'une femme de chambre* into memorable films. Curiously, however, until recent years, the most substantial biographical or critical appraisals of Mirbeau's life and work came from writers outside France: notably, an unpublished doctoral dissertation by J.A. Walker, defended at the University of Toronto in 1954, which offers a critical biography of the writer; another biography by the American Martin Schwarz, published in The Hague in 1966; and a persuasive study of Mirbeau's ideological affinities with anarchism, by Reg Carr, published in Manchester in 1977.

I first encountered the unforgettable bizarreries of *Le Jardin des supplices* and *Le Journal d'une femme de chambre* some twenty years ago, while pursuing the equally decadent extravaganzas of Mirbeau's exact contemporary J.-K. Huysmans. Ten years later, in the mid-1980s, there still seemed to be plenty left to say about Mirbeau as a creator of fictions: hence my undertaking of this book. But as our own fin de siècle approached, I discovered that my interest was increasingly shared by other colleagues and critics (or competitors), whose work in the last decade collectively amounts to a major revaluation of Mirbeau and his age. Unpublished theses have further explored his role as novelist, journalist and art critic, the most substantial being Jean-François Nivet's doctoral dissertation defended at Lyon II in 1987. Subsequently, Nivet joined forces with Pierre Michel to produce the definitive, 1,000-page biography of the author in 1990. This indefatigable team has also edited and published innumerable volumes of Mirbeau's stories, journalism and correspondence, organised scholarly conferences, and overseen publication of the proceedings. In addition, the tireless Michel has relaunched the defunct Société Octave Mirbeau and edits the annual *Cahiers Octave Mirbeau*. As a result, over fifty critical essays on varied aspects of Mirbeau's work have appeared in recent years.

Nevertheless, no book has yet appeared, in French or English, which focuses on Mirbeau as a writer of novels and stories. This is the gap which I hope to fill in this study, whose relatively modest dimensions reflect in part the constraints imposed by the Durham Modern Languages Series, but also my decision to concentrate mainly on the most interesting and innovative aspects of Mirbeau's fiction, the books which he wrote in the second half of his career, in particular *Le Jardin des supplices*, *Le Journal d'une femme de chambre*, *Les 21 Jours d'un neurasthénique* and *La 628–E8*. I have used the term 'fictions' advisedly, since it is less generically restricting than the word novel; the essential point about Mirbeau as a producer of fictions is precisely that, alongside other fin-de-siècle writers, he helps explode the predictable conventions of the naturalist novel laid down and practised by a predecessor like Zola. A further, rather different fiction is that which concerns the identity of the author himself: in the opening chapter, I explore the problems raised by Mirbeau's own questioning of his profession and by Pierre Michel's recent extraordinary extension of the Mirbellian corpus. Subsequent chapters then discuss key themes and techniques such as humour, cruelty, the treatment of social class and biological diversity. My overall aim is to encourage a critical, albeit sympathetic, reading or rereading of Mirbeau's fiction, particularly by those outside France who remain barely aware of his dangerous charms.

This book derives in large part from lectures and papers delivered in France and the United Kingdom between 1989 and 1994, although most chapters have been considerably modified. I am grateful to the editors of *Nineteenth-Century French Studies* and *Salford Occasional Papers in Literary and Cultural Studies* for permission to reproduce the essays now adapted for chapters five and six of this study. References to secondary sources are given in abbreviated form in the text, with full details of publication supplied in the bibliography. The editions of Mirbeau's works cited are the most recent ones listed in the bibliography, except for *Le Journal d'une femme de chambre* and *Les 21 Jours d'un neurasthénique*, where I refer respectively to the versions published by Flammarion (GF) and UGE (10/18).

Finally, I must thank the University of Durham for granting me research leave and funding to assist in the completion of this book, and Joy Newton and Pierre Michel for reading my study in typescript and kindly offering helpful comments and advice.

Chapter One
The Quest for Mirbeau

'En quoi est-on l'auteur de ce que l'on écrit?'
(Pascal Jardin, *La Bête à bon Dieu*)

In a laudable attempt to promote the reputation of Octave Mirbeau, his biographer Pierre Michel has described him as 'Ce Tolstoï français' (*Combats pour l'enfant*, 9). Yet for all his libertarian vigour and imaginative verve, such a grandiose comparison is more likely to cast a deeper shadow over Mirbeau than to illuminate him, either as man or writer. Who was Mirbeau, and how does he appear to us today? What image of the writer does Mirbeau construct for himself, whether as creator of fictions or as journalist committed to social causes? What were the material conditions of his existence, the range of his output? Do we need to ascribe a more prestigious place in the canon to his works (as Michel's analogy suggests), or should we leave his writings to speak for themselves? These are the questions which I would like first to address, before turning to his most interesting and appealing themes and texts in subsequent chapters.

Mirbeau's début was a painful one. The weak-willed hero of his first novel, *Le Calvaire* (1886), refers to his childhood as 'Un long engourdissement', adding: 'tous mes malheurs me sont venus de cette enfance solitaire et morte' (33–35). But it would be ingenuous to yield to the facile temptation of reading the psychological determinism which saps the author's characters as straightforward autobiographical plundering. In point of fact, the sentimental failure of the character Jean Mintié (who departs at the end of the novel, disguised as a worker, and vanishes into the anonymous crowd) corresponded to the professional success of his creator, since the publication of *Le Calvaire* marked the beginning of Mirbeau's reputation as an original novelist; the novel sold some 40,000 copies and earned him 27,000 francs. The first book to which Mirbeau had put his own name had been published at the beginning of the same year. This was the collection of stories, *Lettres de ma chaumière*. Yet at this time, in January 1886, he was nearly thirty-eight years old and had been writing as a journalist in the right-wing press for twelve years.

Mirbeau's biographers present this protracted, venal apprenticeship as a form of slavery. In 1872, he abandoned his menial position as a lawyer's clerk in Rémalard (Orne), where he had been employed for five years (interrupted by military service during the Franco-Prussian war of 1870–71), to become the private secretary of the Bonapartist local deputy Dugué de la Fauconnerie. Apart from a brief period in 1877 as a prefectorial *chef de cabinet* in Foix, for over a decade Mirbeau then remained a paid hack in the service of the Bonapartist and monarchist cause, a defender of the supposed 'moral order' of the early Third Republic. While Mirbeau no doubt shared Flaubert's opinion of the profession of the law as 'une castration morale étrange à concevoir' (*Correspondance*, 1 August 1842; 1973: I, 120), he saw in the journalist an equally emasculated or prostituted figure, ever willing to sell himself to the highest bidder. Although by 1900 Mirbeau had become one of the highest paid journalists of the time and enjoyed considerable financial and intellectual independence, a sense of impotence and moral bankruptcy continued to haunt him; the theme recurs incessantly in all his fictional writings.

The narrator of his last, uncompleted novel, *Un gentilhomme*, presents himself as someone who is 'médiocre et souple' (51). The action of the story returns to the period of President MacMahon's abortive coup d'Etat of 1877: like Mirbeau himself, Charles Varnat has become the secretary of an influential political figure (in this case, a monarchist marquis), and sees himself as an intellectual servant obliged to 'abdiquer le plus de sa personnalité et de sa conscience au service de cet aristocrate réactionnaire' (32). He also informs us that before taking up this disreputable occupation, he moved on the fringes of male prostitution.

Such abject characters bound to an alienating servitude thus feature in Mirbeau's first and last novels, with their obvious autobiographical parallels, as well as in the better-known novels such as *Le Jardin des supplices* and *Le Journal d'une femme de chambre* which mark the high point of his literary career. The failed writer or artist is a more specialised variant on the theme. An early story published in 1882 is called simply 'Un raté'. The main character's name is Jacques Sorel, an obvious derisive reference to the hero of *Le Rouge et le Noir*: for unlike Stendhal's extraordinary *arriviste*, Mirbeau's protagonist is condemned to constant misfortune and obscurity. Michel and Nivet reprint the story in their collection of *Contes cruels* and interpret it as 'une confession voilée' (II,

423). What is the nature of this confession? More seems to be involved here in fact than a straightforward outpouring of personal bitterness. One needs to stress an obvious point: this is not autobiography (a genre which Mirbeau avoids) but fiction, fiction whose autobiographical ingredients are overwritten by the emotional distancing and projection required to produce a convincing story. The author does the opposite of unveiling himself, since the creation of the fictional world allows him to mask his own personality beneath invented characters. Moreover, this particular story also exemplifies the technique of embedded narration which Mirbeau made frequent use of (in novels like *Dans le ciel* and *Le Jardin des supplices*, for example), where any sense of an authorial persona is overlaid by sets of parallel narrators and overlapping stories.

The *I* which recounts the misfortunes of Jacques Sorel is a neutral, anonymous observer who acts as an intermediary and presents what is not so much a confession as a social (or literary) case. Failure is a stock theme in the nineteenth-century novel in France, most famously exemplified by works like Flaubert's *L'Education sentimentale* (1869) and Zola's *L'Œuvre*(1886), and less famously by Huysmans in *En ménage* (1881) and Vallès in *Les Réfractaires* (1865). In this sense, Mirbeau is merely trying his hand at a familiar topic, much as Maupassant does two years later in his better-known story 'Garçon, un bock!' (1884). On closer scrutiny, Jacques Sorel proves to be a somewhat enigmatic character, part confidence trickster (he sometimes lays claim to an aristocratic *particule* or coronet), part unacknowledged genius, capable of knocking out a sonnet as easily as a stock exchange report or suggestive magazine article. He has sacrified himself in order to assist others in making their reputations: 'pour tous j'ai fait des romans, des études d'histoire et de critique, j'ai replâtré des comédies et des drames' (II, 425). His whole existence has made him 'la proie des autres'; he is an author who has been robbed of his works. Yet if he laid claim to the works which others have signed, 'On m'accuserait d'être fou ou un voleur' (426). The narrator closes his story by having Sorel humiliated in the antichamber of a German banker and then leaving him to die, for unspecified causes, in hospital (violent or sudden death tends to serve as a convenient plot device for Mirbeau).

Taking Sorel's complaints at face value, the reader can only assume that he is the victim of misguided altruism or excessive servility. An alternative interpretation would be to see him as prey to paranoiac delusions of grandeur: there is some fantastical about a character who claims to be the invisible agent of other people's success. In an analogous tale called 'Les Millions de Jean Loqueteux' (which also appears in chapter 16 of *Les 21 Jours d'un neurasthénique*), Mirbeau portrays a crazed beggar who thinks he possesses millions (his fortune in fact consists of pebbles). When finally locked up in an asylum, he begins a 'nouvelle carrière de fou — de fou officiel' (*Contes cruels*, I, 231). It seems most likely that in Jacques Sorel's megalomaniac pretensions (he too enjoys 'des heures d'espoirs fous où il se bâtissait des fortunes, des succès et de la gloire' (II,425)), we witness the equivalent in the field of literary creation to the delirious ravings of the old beggar.

Mirbeau's fascination with failure reflects more than a resentful urge for public recognition (in a purely material sense, he himself eventually became a highly rewarded author). What he is questioning is the psychological identity and social function of the writer. If the journalist is a venal lackey, the literary artist is no more than a pale imitator of those who practise the plastic arts; hence his somewhat ambivalent thraldom to artists such as Monet, Pissarro and Rodin, whom he both publicly promoted (casting himself, if not as patron, at least as champion of those unacceptable to conventional canons) and privately adulated to the point of sycophancy. Unsurprisingly, then, Mirbeau can turn even the successful writer into a failure. In a series of satirical dialogues published in *Le Journal* in October and November 1897, Mirbeau invented a character called 'l'Illustre Ecrivain'. His main aim was to ridicule the bad faith and grotesque pretension of a well-known, anti-*dreyfusard* personality and his entourage. As an authoritarian conservative, the illustrious author is inevitably convinced of the social necessity of Dreyfus's guilt, so that the facts or proof of his likely innocence become irrelevant. Just as he is happy for the security of the state to rest upon deceit and repression, so too on closer investigation his own wordly success proves to be based on duplicity. He is in fact the other side of the coin struck by Jacques Sorel, the beneficiary of an 'incroyable mensonge' (*Chez l'illustre écrivain*, 28). In scenes whose grotesque comedy anticipates Ionesco, we discover that the illustrious writer works in collaboration with his valet Joseph, who is the real creator of his celebrated style. His social successes are likewise due to the good works of an *entremetteuse*, Mme Beauduit.

Paul Bourget is often taken as a likely model for this ludicrous charlatan. In the novel *Le Journal d'une femme de chambre*, he is cast as a hypocritical, cold-hearted snob, as opposed to the working-class narrator, whose own unpublished investigations of erotic sensibility prove to be more penetrating and entertaining than those for which Bourget was famous. This is not the place to discuss Bourget's merits or demerits (his relationship with Mirbeau fits a familiar pattern of friendship venomously cast aside by one or both parties), although it is worth recalling that Bourget's most durable novel, *Le Disciple* (1889), also deals with the theme of intellectual responsibility and betrayal. Gide noted sagaciously that what characterised Paul Bourget was an 'absence d'ironie envers soi-même [qui] invitera bien vite, invite déjà, l'ironie du lecteur' (*Journal*, 23 June 1930, I, 991). This distinguishes him from Mirbeau, whose own self-doubts allow him to create an absurdist, hyperbolic manner remote from Bourget's rather solemn and self-regarding tone. (Incidentally, Gide remarked of Mirbeau that 'il retomberait à plat s'il ne s'imaginait environné de monstres' (1 January 1910, I, 290).) For Mirbeau, the writer is constantly made aware of the vain and arbitrary nature of his enterprise and those who glorify it.

In the story 'Un poète local' (1885), the eponymous poet, an uncouth character of dubious talents, is dissatisfied with his 'réputation de clocher' (*Contes cruels*, II, 453), for he considers himself the equal of Zola, Coppée or Hugo. As a result, he has no hesitation in appealing to the supposed authority of the narrator:

> Voyons, monsieur, vous écrivez dans les journaux, par conséquent, vous êtes une force, vous avez de l'influence auprès des directeurs, des acteurs, vous connaissez Coquelin ... Que me faut-il de plus? ... Vous n'avez qu'un mot à dire, et toutes les portes me sont ouvertes ... (453)

These lines are doubly ironical. In the early 1880s, Mirbeau was far from being an opener of doors, and is thus mocking both the inflated aspirations of the poet and the equally fragile glory of his narrator; yet a decade or so later, the role of artistic go-between was one that the writer was increasingly called upon to play, as his promotion of Maeterlinck, Rodin, Charles-Louis Philippe or Marguerite Audoux demonstrates.

In Mirbeau's aesthetic hierarchy, the actor comes somewhat lower than the journalist. He knew Coquelin, but this did not prevent him from launching a vituperative attack on the acting profession in *Le Figaro* in October 1882. It was the rapidity and immediacy of the actor's success that offended the writer, as well as the flagrant exhibitionism of his performance. Twenty years after, when he had become a successful playwright (and married a former actress), Mirbeau belatedly withdrew his strictures. Personal envy was thus an obvious motive for the attack, but it also reflects the writer's hostile and confused perception of the social hierarchy and its effect on individual identity. He perceives the actor as 'un être inférieur et un réprouvé', who by displaying himself on stage 'a fait l'abdication de sa qualité d'homme'; nonetheless, 'par une aberration de la responsabilité sociale', the performer usurps 'dans la vie une place qui ne lui appartient pas' ('Le Comédien', *Combats politiques*, 46).

Coquelin in fact replied to Mirbeau's article a few days later in *Le Temps* (1 November 1882), requesting him to 'rabaisser le ton de plusieurs *octaves*' and reminding him that not only actors but all artists are perceived to be 'en représentation' and take on a public persona (*Le Comédien*, 1883: 6, 9). Mirbeau probably would not have disputed the point; in the polemical journal *Les Grimaces* which he was editing the following year, he denounced the corruption of the press and the journalist, 'devenu machine à louange et à éreintement, comme la fille publique, machine à plaisir; seulement, celle-ci ne livre que sa chair, tandis que celui-là livre toute son âme' (29 September 1883; quoted in *Lettres à Bansard*, 30, n.10). Whether Mirbeau included himself in this category is unclear, although it seems likely. The aggressive posture which he adopted towards the powerful and famous once he had achieved a measure of independence as a journalist in the mid-1880s is in fact matched in private by an equally sceptical inspection and display of his own personal inadequacies.

He admits to Monet in 1888 that 'je ne suis pas un homme de génie, pas même un homme [de] talent' (*Correspondance avec Monet*, 61). He laments that *Le Calvaire* 'est une œuvre ratée, et vide, et que j'aurais voulu très intense, et qui n'est, dans le fond, que déclamatoire ... Je ferais bien mieux de confectionner des bottes' (*Correspondance avec Rodin*, 60). In 1891, he can do no better than 'produire des choses qui ne viennent pas, ou si vagues, si lointaines, si inutiles! [...] Mais l'impuissance est au fond de moi' (*Correspondance avec Pissarro*, 56). In fact, Mirbeau did not produce a book for eight years in the 1890s (apart from a revised collection of stories, *Contes de la chaumière*, in 1894). The novel *Dans le ciel* which he wrote at this time is a drama of artistic impotence. It was serialised in twenty-eight instalments in *L'Echo de Paris* from 20 September 1892 to 2 May 1893, but never subsequently revised for publication as a book (until resurrected by Michel and Nivet in 1989, having been partially reprinted in the posthumous collection of stoies *La Pipe de cidre* in 1919). The most memorable character in *Dans le ciel* is an artist tormented by his creative inadequacy. The painter Lucien illustrates his sterility by describing a recurrent nightmare which afflicts him:

> Je suis un jardinier, et je plante des lys. A mesure que j'approche de la terre le bulbe puissant et beau comme un sexe, il se fane, dans ma main, les écailles s'en détachent, pourries et gluantes, et lorsque je veux enfin l'enfouir dans le sol, le bulbe a disparu; tous mes rêves ont le même caractère de l'avortement, de la pourriture, de la mort! (121)

To achieve his goal, then, the artist must couple with the earth, be fecundated by nature, become part of a biological cycle. Yet Lucien shies away from sexuality, which he sees as a 'sale blague' and an 'acte idiot' (124), rather than as a form of erotic fulfilment. And at the same time his aesthetic ambitions are both overweening and absurd: he yearns to paint 'Un grand ciel ... Et l'aboi de ce chien! ...' (125). His excoriating lucidity forces him to confess that that he is incapable of painting the simplest object and that 'C'est pour masquer mon impuissance que je vais cherchant toutes les folies dont je meurs' (130). Finally he cuts off the right hand which has treacherously refused to carry out his will, before committing suicide.

To link the subject matter of this failed novel to its author's career again requires a certain delicacy and the recognition of its paradoxical status. Mirbeau is a successful author writing about an unsuccessful painter. To this can be added the critical distance achieved by his use of a separate second narrator, himself presented by a first narrator. This first character briefly visits the desolate hill-top place, 'dans le ciel', inhabited by his comrade Georges, whom he has not seen for fifteen years, which allows Georges to hand over the manuscript recounting his own dealings with the painter Lucien. The embedded narrative is as clumsy and half-hearted as this summary may suggest. Georges is oddly called 'X' at the beginning of the story, as though Mirbeau had little desire to name what he calls this 'silencieux insecte' (ch. 8). The character closest to the author is obviously the first, anonymous narrator, who appears to lead a comfortable existence in Paris, rather than the provincial exiles Georges and Lucien. There is an obvious parallel with Zola's earlier novel *L'Œuvre*(1886), with its contrasting suicidal painter Claude Lantier and more stable writer Pierre Sandoz, although a more immediate model for a painter afflicted by self-mutilation and bouts of insanity was Van Gogh, who died in 1891. (For further details, see the essay published by Joy Newton in 1991.) Van Gogh also demonstrates the paradox of failure transformed into posthumous glory (the reverse of Paul Bourget, from our perspective).

It is evident that a writer who publishes over twenty books and hundreds of newspaper articles can hardly be suspected of creative impotence. Facile biographical identifications are thus unhelpful. But the fact remains that the plot of *Dans le ciel* is matched by the conditions of its actual publication. Mirbeau earned 8,400 francs for the weekly serial, but his reluctance to give the work a less ephemeral existence outside the pages of a newspaper suggests that he saw it as an abortive production. What troubled him, no doubt, was not so much the mirage of professional acclamation, as the betrayal of a personal ideal. This was the reason why he particularly despised the compromises which he thought Zola had committed in his search for glory in the 1890s (although, typically, Mirbeau reversed his position to one of admiration when the author of *L'Argent* and *La Débâcle* sacrificed his reputation for the sake of Captain Dreyfus). Thus he wrote to his fellow anarchist sympathiser Pissarro in September 1891:

> Et que dites-vous de Zola, qui défend l'idée de la guerre! Quel méprisable bonhomme! Pour de méchantes vanités, il aura tout renié de ce qu'il défendait autrefois. Il trouve que l'argent et que le capital sont admirables; il trouve que tout est pour le mieux dans notre société. Tout va bien parce qu'il gagne de l'argent! (*Correspondance avec Pissarro*, 36)

* * *

Writing back to Mirbeau, and wanting perhaps to console him, Camille Pissarro observed that 'Quand je prends la plume ou le crayon, plus rien, rien, je vous assure, je suis idiot' (*Correspondance avec Pissarro*, 98 n.2).

Mirbeau himself was not troubled by Mallarmé's 'le vide papier que la blancheur défend', but rather the opposite: like the author of the *Rougon-Macquart*, he was threatened by literary overproduction, a sort of verbal inflation where as words proliferate they have less and less value. He asked Pissarro in 1891 to excuse his silence, for 'Je travaille comme un nègre, je m'essouffle, je halète' (56), yet without ever achieving the quality of work he has set himself. As Pierre Michel observes

L'impuissance n'est pas pour lui, une incapacité à écrire, mais, au contraire, et paradoxalement, une trop grande facilité acquise par des années de métier. Or le métier est à ses yeux l'arme des médiocres. Et il avait sans doute bien des réticences face à une œ uvre composée à la hâte, avec le souci de se débarrasser au plus vite de l'horrible corvée que représente la chronique hebdomadaire à date fixe.

(*Octave Mirbeau*, 1992: 205)

Pierre Michel's recent discoveries have added new weight to this view of Mirbeau chained to his desk like the 'nègre' or ghostwriter of literary legend. In a lecture given in 1991 (and subsequently published in the proceedings of the *Colloque Octave Mirbeau* which came out in 1994), Michel claimed that Mirbeau spent much of the early 1880s revising or composing fifteen or more books which then appeared as the work of other writers. This discovery is a surprising one for readers and critics of Mirbeau who assumed that they knew and understood the range of his works and the place they give him in fin-de-siècle literature: that is, as a writer whose most effective books combine social libertarianism, decadent naturalism and caustic black humour, while breaking free of the more ponderous narrative and psychological conventions of the nineteenth-century realist novel. Apart from anything else, Michel's revelation of Mirbellian apocrypha effectively doubles the number of fictional works which he was thought to have written. It also reveals how little we may really know about an author removed from us by no more than three generations.

There can be little doubt that all students of Octave Mirbeau owe an immense debt to the scholarly labours of Jean-François Nivet and Pierre Michel, the compilers of a massive, authoritative biography of the writer published in 1990 and the editors of his correspondence (still in course of publication). In the widest sense, by publishing innumerable collections of texts by Mirbeau and by creating a forum for critical debate in conferences and academic publications, they have brought this author back to public attention. And in a narrower (perhaps more useful) way, they have corrected many of the errors committed by earlier biographers. Such errors have made the writer a figure of legend rather than historical reality; surprisingly, many of them are still perpetuated in recent editions of his works. Before confronting the bibliographical problems raised by Michel's extension of the Mirbeau corpus, it would be useful to raise some of the biographical queries which still remain unresolved. The quest for Mirbeau's identity as a writer can be a frustrating one.

There are simple errors, of course. Thus the cover of a reprint of *Dingo* (1987) shows a drawing of a long-eared dog which looks suspiciously like a spaniel, despite the antipodean origins of the novel's canine hero. More seriously, as far as the author's own life is concerned, in a reprint of the *Contes de la chaumière* (1987), Thierry Maricourt states that Mirbeau was born in 1850 and the son of a notary. In fact, he was born on 16 February 1848, and his father was an *officier de santé* (like Flaubert's Charles Bovary). The biographical chronology printed in Gallimard's 'Folio' editions of *Le Jardin des supplices* (1988) and *Le Journal d'une femme de chambre* (1984) erroneously relates Mirbeau's wife Alice Regnault to her more famous namesake, the actress Jeanne-Julia Regnault, a *sociétaire* of the Comédie-Française better known as Julia Bartet. This imaginary sisterhood is all the more surprising, since Albert Fournier showed in a solidly documented article published in 1967 that Alice Regnault's real name was Augustine Alexandrine Toulet. She was born on 5 February 1849, and first married a mechanic called Jules Renard in 1865; they had a son, Edouard, in 1866 (who died at the age of twenty-five in 1892). Renard himself died in 1868, and for the next decade Alice became an actress, acquiring a reputation as a cocotte and considerable wealth. She did in fact lose custody of her son after Renard's death, supposedly because of her dissolute existence (Nivet and Michel, 1990: 216). She probably cohabited with Mirbeau from 1883 and they married in May 1887. She outlived him by fourteen years, dying in July 1931. Biographers continue to cast Mirbeau's spouse as a mercenary, avaricious woman, whose supposedly disreputable past had made her into a ungenerous and inhibited character clinging relentlessly to her bourgeois respectability. Such interpretations are, however, largely speculative, and reveal an unpleasant, misogynist bias, which derives from Mirbeau himself and chroniclers such as Edmond de Goncourt.

There is no doubt that Mirbeau and his wife were extremely wealthy, especially from the turn of the century, when his fame as journalist, playwright and novelist was undisputed; they rented or owned large properties in the provinces and Paris, ran highly expensive motor cars, and employed a retinue of domestics, chauffeurs and gardeners to service their needs. The catalogues published of Mirbeau's library and art collection after his death show the extent both of his tastes and his riches. Yet the source of either Octave or Alice Mirbeau's wealth still remains something of a mystery, since it seems to have exceeded whatever they might have legitimately earned from, respectively, writing or the stage.

Equally mysterious, and more relevant to Mirbeau as a creator of fictions — whether in life or literature — are the existence and authorship of some his works, a problem which has now been greatly magnified by Pierre Michel's discoveries. Bibliographies of his writings almost invariably include a book of drama criticism, entitled *Le Pour et le Contre*, supposedly published in 1887. In fact no one has ever set eyes on a copy of this work, which never featured in the *Catalogue général de la librairie française*. In an edition of *Le Journal d'une femme de chambre* published by Livre de poche (1986: 477), Daniel Leuwers claims that Mirbeau published a work called *Les Amies, scènes d'amour saphique* in 1866 (this was the year he took the baccalauréat, aged eighteen). It is more likely that this is a spicy book by Verlaine. The same editor also inflicts a twenty-month sentence in a military prison on the unfortunate Octave in 1871–72 (he was in fact accused of desertion in 1871, though eventually acquitted), not to mention a further envigorating eighteen months which he supposedly spent in 1878–79 working in the sardine fishing industry.

Such blunders are forgivable, perhaps inevitable, when trying to come to terms with an author whose career contains strange gaps and shadows. Indeed, the contemporary reader is indebted to those publishers and editors who have been willing to make his works available in accessible editions, whatever their lapses. Although Nivet and Michel's biography runs to over 1,000 pages, their very success in documenting his existence and dismissing certain persistent legends ultimately tends to reinforce one's impression that in many ways Mirbeau is curiously unknowable. As has already been suggested, areas which remain opaque are his financial situation (like Balzac, Mirbeau earned a great deal, but apparently spent even more); the boundaries of his written output; and his relationship with Alice Regnault (not to mention the infamous Judith Vimmer who preceded her).

How did Mirbeau pay off the debts of 150,000 francs which he had somehow contracted by 1886? Who was Judith Vimmer, described by Jean-François Nivet as 'une rousse horizontale' (*Croquis bretons*, 12), who sapped Mirbeau's existence in 1882–83? (Not merely, one hopes, a retrospective extrapolation concocted by inventive biographers from the femme fatale Juliette in *Le Calvaire*; in fact her existence is documented in Mirbeau's letters to Hervieu, which feature in the first volume of the forthcoming edition of his correspondence.) Such questions, regrettably, fall outside the scope of a study whose main goal is to offer a thematic reading of Mirbeau's fictional writing. Issues of bibliographic attribution are evidently more relevant. We obviously need to know where Mirbeau's work starts and finishes. Here again, we might distinguish articles published in the press from actual books, which one would normally expect to remain more accessible and less ephemeral.

The most straightforward way to investigate Mirbeau's journalistic output is to refer to the magisterial unpublished doctoral thesis which Jean-François Nivet defended on this topic at the University of Lyon II in 1987. (It should be noted that his bibliography of sources and of Mirbeau's articles, running to 148 pages, was unfortunately not reproduced in the subsequent biography co-authored with Pierre Michel.) Nivet enumerates 1,185 contributions by Mirbeau to about forty newspapers and reviews between 1875 and 1917. In other words, over a period of forty-two years, Mirbeau wrote about thirty newspaper articles a year, apart from his plays and novels. In fact, his journalistic output was not evenly spread over his career; he was most productive in the two decades running from 1883 to 1901, writing on average fifty articles a year. Moreover, these figures probably rather underestimate his productivity. In a paper given at Angers in 1991, Nivet quoted the figure of 1,500 articles. And in Pierre Michel's view, Nivet's inventory may represent only half of what the author actually wrote: apart from the fifteen or so volumes which he may have ghosted, the indefatigable journalist could have written another thousand articles under a variety of pseudonyms.

As was common practice at the time, Mirbeau used various pseudonyms in the journals to which he contributed (sometimes this was an editorial requirement, when a writer had given his name to a rival organ). Pseudonyms which have been identified as Mirbeau's include Henry Lys, Jean Maure, Daniel René, Nirvana, Montrevêche, le Diable. The question of course arises, to which it is difficult to give a convincing answer: how can one identify with absolute certainty the real author of a pseudonymous or anonymous work? In Mirbeau's case, it needs to be recalled that not only did he write many unsigned texts, at the beginning of his career, but also that towards the end certain works which were published under his name may well have been written in collaboration with other writers (notably *Le Foyer* and *Dingo*, and possibly even *La 628–E8*). In addition, the authenticity of his posthumous 'Testament politique' has long been contested; the jingoistic tone of this final pronouncement suggests it was concocted by his spouse and her entourage, unless of course the author, who made something of a show of his ideological twists and turns, had decided to abandon his pacifist anarchism as he gave his last breath.

Inevitably, then, one approaches Pierre Michel's account of Mirbeau's spectral career as a ghostwriter with a measure of scepticism. To give a full account of the many volumes which may have poured from the writer's pen would obviously require a further volume in itself, an enterprise which I prefer to leave to future commentators. At this stage, it seems more appropriate to rehearse the evidence as presented by Michel, to allow readers to judge for themselves whether to add the books in question to the Mirbellian canon. An opening observation is that the use of *nègres* was a common practice in the nineteenth century, and continues to this day (famous literary examples include Dumas père and Willy, and a lesser one the actress Marie Colombier, who exploited the talents of Paul Bonnetain and Paul Adam). An objection which arises immediately, in my view, is that such examples of course illustrate the *transparency* of the practice, whereas in Mirbeau's case the secret had been preserved for over a century.

In passing, it is worth noting that Mme Mirbeau also wrote newspaper articles, in 1884, and published two uninspiring novels in 1886 and 1888; she also produced an unpublished play, *La Cadette*, which some biographers have attributed to her husband. One does indeed wonder whether Mirbeau may have had a hand in the writing of these texts.

Looking at the writer's earliest, official writings, Michel then draws attention to the character of the much-abused author presented in 'Un raté', although, as we have seen, to see this as autobiographical is purely speculative. In fact the most solid piece of evidence which Michel can muster is a letter from Mirbeau to the publisher Ollendorff, probably written in March 1885; in this, he refers to two novels, one just published, the other in page proofs which he is correcting. (See 'Quand Mirbeau faisait «le nègre»', *Colloque Octave Mirbeau*, 1994: 83.) It is most regrettable that Pierre Michel chooses neither to quote the text of this hitherto unknown letter nor to explain its provenance, since the rest of his argument effectively springs from this one piece of evidence. As a result, it is impossible to know in just what terms Mirbeau describes his activity as a clandestine author.

However, even if we take this letter in good faith, it appears that Mirbeau may have written or contributed to one or two books which were published under other names. How do we move from this hypothesis to ascribing to the writer the authorship of another dozen volumes in the period 1880–86 (apart from the substantial body of journalistic work he completed at the same time)? The leap seems a hazardous one, and in fact Michel's argument becomes least convincing when he cites the titles of the works in question. Between 1880 and 1886, then, Mirbeau is supposed to have used four pseudonyms (which Pierre Michel has tracked down by systematically trawling through Ollendorff's records and the *Catalogue général de la librairie française*): Albert Miroux, Alain Bauquenne, Forsan, and Jeanne Mairet. Is it by sheer chance that the first syllables of the names Miroux and Bauquenne form 'Mir-Bau', or is this a surreptitious onomastic hint from our author? (The names Michel and Nivet can likewise be fused to form 'Michelet', but perhaps that is a different story....)

Albert Miroux was the author of a single book, called *Les Défaillances: Jean Marcellin*, published by Ollendorff in 1885. In actual fact, this particular novel had previously been attributed to Mirbeau, both in the Bibliothèque Nationale catalogue and Talvart and Place's standard bibliography of French literature. On the other hand, the *Catalogue général de la librairie française* describes Miroux as a 'littérateur, né à Paris en 1861', and Michel points out that there is a manuscript note added to the endpaper of the copy of *Jean Marcellin* kept in the Bibliothèque de l'Arsenal: 'L'éditeur a fait connaître que l'auteur de *Jean Marcellin* est Albert Miroux et non O. Mirbeau, indiqué par erreur sur le titre intérieur'. As for Alain Bauquenne, he was the pseudonymous author of seven books published by Ollendorff between 1880 and 1885; according to the Bibliothèque Nationale catalogue, his real name was André Bertera (or Bertéra). Pierre Michel has succeeded in tracking down a birth certificate for Paul-André Bertéra, who was born in Marnes-la-Coquette on 24 June 1853, but left no subsequent traces. The pseudonyms Forsan and Jeanne Mairet belonged to two women writers who also certainly existed: the first, of Italian origin, was called Dora Melegari, and the second, of American origin, Mary Healy. A work by Forsan, *Dans la vieille rue* (Ollendorff, 1885), is the one explicitly mentioned by Mirbeau in his letter to the publisher.

As things stand, we are thus a long way from possessing formal proof of the role played by Mirbeau in writing these books, as Pierre Michel is forced to admit: for instance, 'Pour les trois romans signés Jeanne Mairet, l'attribution à Mirbeau ne repose sur aucune preuve extérieure, mais seulement sur l'ensemble des présomptions internes à l'œ uvre' (87). What about all the other books which Jeanne Mairet then wrote — more than a dozen, which Michel somewhat tendentiously does not mention in his account? But ultimately, the issue is less one of authorship (perhaps unprovable) than of the interest of the newly-discovered texts. Unlike Pierre Michel, I must confess to a feeling of great disappointment on skimming through the copies of the supposed 'romans nègres' available in the British Library in London. We are, I suppose, driven to read and write about Mirbeau because we find that he has something novel to offer and yet often passes unnoticed in the crowd of more celebrated authors. I doubt that any unprejudiced reader is likely to be stirred by the pages of Miroux or Bauquenne, whoever they were. Pierre Michel remarks apologetically of his pseudo-Mirbeau that 'écrivant sous un nom d'emprunt, soumis aux exigences de ses commanditaires, il n'en est pas encore à entreprendre des recherches originales et à frayer des voies nouvelles' (96). In other words, this Mirbeau bears little relation to the author of *Le Calvaire* or *La 628–E8*, whether stylistically or thematically.

I confess that my reading of these dozen problematic texts was fairly superficial (since Pierre Michel intends to republish some of them, readers will eventually be able to make their own minds up). Flicking through the opening pages of *Jean Marcellin*, one comes across an idealised description of Jean's cousin, Marguerite de Hauterive, duchesse de Herbeumont, which concludes with the phrase 'Sous le corsage souple deux seins, petits, élastiques, dressaient leurs splendeurs jumelles' (10), to which can be added the appeal of her 'belle voix de cristal' (13). In Bauquenne's *La Belle Madame Le Vassart* (1884), that famous cliché of romantic literature makes an unashamed appearance: 'Leurs yeux se rencontrèrent' (38). No doubt this rough-and-ready method of sampling stylistic commonplaces and social stereotypes has its dangers; Gide earned himself the derision of posterity for dismissing *Du côté de chez Swann* in a similar fashion. The risk does not seem very great here. Besides, such examples could be multiplied with little difficulty, if the effort was worth it. If Mirbeau never owned up to these books, perhaps it was because he never actually wrote them; or if he did, was either contractually prevented from claiming their authorship, or, in some cases at least, was ashamed to admit it. Their anonymity seems to me to reflect their true value, and I would prefer, from now on, to turn to the works which made the writer's reputation, while accepting that his status as an author is likely to remain problematic for the foreseeable future.

Chapter Two
Humour, Cruelty, Caricature

> What Humor is, not all the Tribe
> Of Logick-Mongers can describe.
> (Swift)

Despite the renewed interest in Mirbeau's works which critics have shown since the late 1980s, most still perceive the writer as an ideological polemicist or combative journalist rather than as an original creator. The fact that he is a comic author is often overlooked altogether, although black humour, the grotesque and caricature are the main weapons in his verbal arsenal. A more detailed overview of these aspects of his writing serves as a useful and necessary preamble to discussion of individual books, providing one heeds Swift's warning about logic-chopping definitions.

Does Mirbeau actually make us laugh? A rapid glance at a few samples of his humour will show whether our own fin de siècle still responds to the same emotional resonances as its predecessor. One could take as a starting point Sébastien Roch, a type or stereotype of the disaffected adolescent, whose abortive education concludes the trilogy of novels which mark Mirbeau's early manner (that is, *Le Calvaire, L'Abbé Jules, Sébastien Roch*: each book constitutes a fictional biography with some connection to the author's own adolescence, with a realistic social setting to some extent undercut by the narrator's satirical programme). In a wider context, the eponymous hero of *Sébastien Roch* is an avatar of all the abulic protagonists of naturalist novels who are invariably crushed by their milieu: in his case, he becomes the victim of his father, the Jesuits, and finally warfare, while being simultaneously undermined from within by less manifest forces, 'l'infiltration continue de son vice' (349), as the narrator puts it, striking a moralising tone akin to that of Paul Bonnetain in his notorious fictionalised study of onanism, *Charlot s'amuse*, published seven years earlier in 1883. In both novels, the enterprise of investigating sexual vice in a spirit of sententious righteousness is likely to strike the modern reader as potentially laughable. The very lack of gaiety in Sébastien's lugubrious provincial existence may seem to suggest parody of the schematic sleaze of the naturalist case study. His complaints about the disturbing influence of the wallpaper in his room reveal a neurasthenic aestheticism best expressed by Huysmans' des Esseintes in *A rebours* a few years earlier (though Proust's narrator, who likewise makes a room into an extension of the self, is also anticipated here, as he often is in Mirbeau's portrayal of tortured sensibilities). But the obsession with dirt and decay is overdone, forcing us to read them ironically as self-conscious literary devices which deride the doleful mannerisms of the genre.

For instance, the Roch family housekeeper, la mère Cébron, is 'infiniment malpropre', as she conclusively demonstrates by washing a pair of stockings which she has worn for a month in the coffee pot (287). Hence perhaps the French expression for undrinkable coffee: 'jus de chaussette'. This bizarre culinary exercise is doubly comic: the receptacle patently does not fit the purpose it is used for, while the month-old stockings recall the hoary joke (which Freud nonetheless analyses at ponderous length in *Jokes and their Relation to the Unconscious*) about the Victorian person who took a bath once a month, whether dirty or not. In Mirbeau's fictional world of crumbling naturalism, even the quest for cleanliness serves to confirm the inherently filthy and contaminated state in which his characters subsist. Humour, however incidental, is rarely innocent, and usually double-edged: while it pleases or distracts, it also disturbs or sickens. Like many of his contemporaries, the writer is not averse to scatological comedy, whose coarseness usually betrays an unsavoury fascination with malfunctioning physiology. Mirbeau breaks taboos, though he sets limits to his excesses in this area. His humour is provocative and equivocal (hence Degas's description of him as a pyromaniac fireman), sadistic (in Hubert Juin's words, 'il aime les cruautés de ses fantoches' (preface to *Les 21 Jours d'un neurasthénique*, 11)), but also euphemistic.

Unlike, say, Alphonse Allais, Mirbeau never set out to be a professional comic writer. In other words his intention was not to 'faire rire à tout prix et par n'importe quel détour' (Grojnowski & Sarrazin, 1990: 23) or to become a 'virtuose du texte court' (Defays, 1991: 279). His overtly comic stories and articles are not always very successful. An exception might be made for a fanciful short text like 'Le Concombre fugitif' (1894), which celebrates a père Hortus and his 'plantes qui font des blagues'. The roving cucumber does not actually appear, resplendently long, round and green, until the final sentence when it flashes past before disappearing in the undergrowth. The sequel, 'Explosif et baladeur', offers a fuller description of the vegetable protagonist warding off hunters by spitting seeds in their face; this time Mirbeau signals that he is in comic mode by dedicating the story explicitly to Alphonse Allais. Despite the aggressive antics of the plant and the crazy behaviour of the gardener, we are a long way from the horrors of *Le Jardin des supplices*, even if the narrator is left mystified by this ambulant vegetable, which is 'insaisissable et diabolique'. This sort of ludic, comic writing is unusual for Mirbeau. Working through his texts, one can however easily find less sustained examples of jokes and puns. Remaining in the vegetable kingdom, the narrator of *Le Jardin des supplices* stands for Parliament as a 'candidat betteravier' (66) (mangled by the farming lobby) or defines a *cocotier* (coconut palm) as an 'arbre à cocottes [...une] classification bien parisienne' (108). Likewise, the surname of Célestine's employers in *Le Journal d'une femme de chambre*, Lanlaire, seems mainly chosen to allow a facile pun ('Va te faire lanlaire!', 57); similarly, the famous lawyer Me du Buit in *Les 21 Jours d'un neurasthénique*, 'dont la tête glabre et bise semble être taillée dans la même matière que son nom', or the bust of Victor Hugo which bursts 'en mille éclats de rire' (95, 94) allow straightforward word play. Again, in *Le Foyer*, the institution serves to 'détourner les mineures ... du vice' (34–35) (the joke depends on the characteristic use of the three dots as a caesura), while the narrator of *La 628–E8* informs a languorous lady he has never loved in Venice: 'Dois-je dire [...] que je me gondolais?' (259).

Evidently, a mere listing of all Mirbeau's wordplays, allusions and quips does not take us very far. Not only do these examples suffer in their translation from the author's page, but also the modern reader — especially a foreign reader — can never be entirely certain of having grasped all the nuances, even when jokes look fairly simple. In *La 628–E8*, the chauffeur Brossette remarks with chauvinistic sagacity: 'Les Allemands, monsieur? ... quel peuple de sauvages! ... Ils ne comprennent pas un mot de français ...' (83). Humour too has its language, a rhetoric and ideology very characteristic of a particular author and his age. It is quite possible that we no longer really understand what amused the readers of the Belle Epoque. On the other hand, if Mirbeau outlives the limits of turn-of-the-century humour and continues to divert and trouble us, this is perhaps convincing evidence of the vigour and universality of his writing.

Humour is a polemical weapon, but also a stylistic and psychological device. Mirbeau's humour is aggressive and tendentious; mystification is a key element. The knife can be turned against the aggressor and become a means of defence or evasion, often at the expense of the reader who is left bemused. Mirbeau's laughter is unpleasant, the smile giving way to the grimace (a favourite word or expression in his lexicon), with all its connotations of ataxia or reification. To laugh at someone is to denigrate and deride him in a moral sense, and to defile him almost physically. Thus Sébastien Roch, the ironmonger's son surrounded by the insolent offspring of the provincial nobility at his school in Vannes ('Tu es venu ici pour rétamer des casseroles, dis?') is wounded by 'un éclat de rire, une explosion de moqueries qui lui éclaboussaient la figure, ainsi qu'un jet de boue' (104). Typically, the pot-bellied priest supervising the schoolboys joins in the mockery of a social inferior, betraying both his paternal and Christian mission.

A smile can indeed suffice to betray the spiritual baseness of those who serve the establishment; witness the 'sourire insidieux de mauvais prêtre' which Sébastien observes 'dans les plis ignobles [des] lèvres mal rasées' of the brother charged with guarding him, after his betrayal at the hands of Father de Kern (246). This unshaven face symbolises uncleanliness and barely repressed sensuality (hence the expression 'mal rasé comme un frère de collège' which occurs later in the book (290)). The remainder of the portrait is in keeping with the initial impression: a servile back and devious look, an 'odeur combinée de latrine et de chapelle', not forgetting the 'pantalon [qui] tombe en plis crapuleux sur des chaussons de misère' (246). The notion that an ill-fitting pair of trousers is a sufficient indicator of debauchery is a pleasing form of physiognomical shorthand, which recalls Robbe-Grillet's observation that a waistcoat in Balzac often acquires a personality in its own right.

The victim can however retaliate by using derision against his adversaries. This is the case in *Le Journal d'une femme de chambre*, where the chambermaid Célestine is one of Mirbeau's livelier characters and plays the alternate roles of mistress and slave. Her journal of course gives her the verbal armoury of the writer. Nonetheless, Célestine eventually realises that her joyful perception of sordid doings above and below stairs offers at best 'une sorte de sécurité crapuleuse', a 'rictus servile', a 'goût de l'ordure passionnelle' normally to be found 'chez le comédien, le juge et le valet' (167). This is 'l'amère grimace de la révolte, le pli dur et crispé du sarcasme'; such laughter 'brûle et dessèche' (177). Used as a form of defence, laughter may thus create an alienated personality caught in the trap of its own grimaces; to unmask others, one needs oneself to wear a clown's mask. Such criticism was levelled at the author himself: Sarcey could see in the play *Les Mauvais Bergers* only the tritest commonplaces, 'de l'imagerie d'Epinal', while the concluding massacre had all the pathos of a knockabout puppet show, in his view (1901: 314, 325). Characters like the abbé Jules and Clara may well be 'de grandes figures ricanantes', in Michel Delon's words (*Le Jardin des supplices*, 8), but insane frenzy is in the end a poor substitute for simpler and subtler study of behaviour. The abbé Jules starts and finishes as 'une indéchiffrable énigme', a mystifier, a 'parodiste de sa propre personnalité' inventing 'des farces lugubres [...] pour tromper l'immense ennui de son existence' (*L'Abbé Jules*, 63, 77, 82, 102)

Mirbeau's humour, then, frequently becomes a vehicle for his pessimism. Nevertheless, comedy can also have a more positive function, particularly from a formal point of view. Humour is the glue which prevents texts that become more and more fragmented from falling apart. To what extent does the writer avoid the monotony induced by overworking the same tricks and devices and the risk of being hoist by his own petard, like the proverbial pyromaniac fireman? If we recapitulate the most striking aspects of his comic technique, as illustrated by some of the preceding examples, we see that excess, hyperbole and caricature are all employed as satirical means to ridicule and provoke real or imagined adversaries. A more playful purely verbal humour is also used, often in the form of similes or metaphors which deliberately subvert the verisimilitude of realist description, especially in more overtly parodic pieces. (For instance, the pre-Raphaelite painter who collects English umbrellas which are 'fins comme des cigares et nus comme des filles' (*Des artistes*, 53).) At the same time, the writer's silences and hesitations can be as significant as his comic and sadistic excesses, since they raise the question of what limits can be set on the representation of horror or obscenity.

Before I examine the writer's caricatural repertory, some comment on the cruelty and overstatement for which he is notorious seems appropriate. For all the prurience and scandal-seeking of his work, Mirbeau can hardly be termed an immoralist. In fact it makes more sense to see him as a puritan who uses humour and exaggeration to contain the horror or timidity aroused in him by the physical or physiological functions of the human being. It is difficult to find a genuinely pornographic or erotic scene in his writings, if by this one means a scene presenting sexual acts explicitly with the intention of arousing the reader. Like the Marquis de Sade, Mirbeau links black humour and cruelty, but he has none of Sade's pornographic relish when he describes an act of debauchery, and none of Sade's curious urge to quantify the voluminous proportions and erotic feats of his protagonists. Thus when Mirbeau describes the homosexual seduction of Sébastien Roch by Father de Kern, the act of sodomy is never mentioned, but suggested by a hiatus in the text. Admittedly, Mirbeau refers more facetiously to this episode in a private letter to Monet, when he begs forgiveness for his silence on the grounds that he has been distracted by the need to 'faire violer un enfant par un jésuite' (*Correspondance avec Monet*, 73). But in his public texts, Mirbeau's discourse on vice and sexuality is nearly always moralising and indirect. In *Sébastien Roch*, the rape becomes the 'meurtre d'une âme d'enfant' (211).

Despite his anticlerical materialism, traces of a morbid Christianity can be detected in Mirbeau's works, where the body is both sacred vessel and source of guilt (compare titles like *Le Calvaire* or its projected sequel, *Rédemption*). Anything which penetrates the body's defences is an occasion of fascination and danger (this largely sums up the programme of *Le Jardin des supplices*). Loss of vital fluids is equally perilous: the torture of the caress in *Le Jardin des supplices* involves a session of enforced masturbation which eventually results in the victim's demise. Humour allows a closer approach to forbidden territory, while relieving the tension caused by exploration of taboo areas. Certain jokes, however salacious, actually depend on litotes. For instance, what can there be inside the little box which Célestine's mistress obstinately refuses to open for an insistent customs officer at the Belgian frontier? To name the object would be to spoil the surprise effect, either for the reader or startled customs man who exclaims when it is at last revealed: 'Fallait le dire que vous étiez veuve!' In fact, he is so astonished at the sight of these family jewels that he leaps backwards 'comme s'il avait eu peur d'être mordu par une bête venimeuse' (*Le Journal d'une femme de chambre*,131). The phallus may be unnameable, but even a dildo's bite is worse than its bark.

Jean-Claude Carrière suggests that black humour 'consiste à rire de la mort' (1988: 333). For Mirbeau, a living body is already close to a cadaver. A little Breton maidservant has legs 'si courtes qu'on pouvait la prendre pour une cul-de-jatte' and 'une peau grise, squameuse, une peau de couleuvre morte' (*Le Journal d'une femme de chambre*, 312). Her filthiness is more predictable, but with certain gestures Mirbeau gives the physically grotesque a sort of sublime absurdity; for example, 'Elle enfouit le pouce dans les profondes cavernes de son nez' (314). Such details explode the conventional, plausible limits of the human body, and recall Bergson's thesis that we laugh at phenomena which defy expected norms, or more flatly, which suggest a 'trucage mécanique de la vie' (1927: 41–44).

Bergson's examples in the celebrated essay *Le Rire* can be more illuminating than his argument. 'Pourquoi rit-on d'un nègre?' he asks. Answer: because 'Un nègre est un blanc déguisé', a freak of nature comparable to dyed hair, red noses and artificial flowers. Such ethnocentricity may amuse or offend us nowadays. What one might call colonial humour seems to have perished with the Empire (French or British), but clearly formed a recognised genre at the beginning of the twentieth century, when the mission to control inferior races was seen as worthy of praise or derision. For example, a story like Edouard Osmont's 'Mon nègre' shows the narrator trying a variety of methods to whiten the skin of his servant, 'un magnifique Soudanais'. The final solution is to plunge the negro into a vat of nickel and to use him as a paperweight (complete with fig leaf). A dark tale in every sense, since colour prejudice, death and impeccable bad taste are skilfully united (the piece was first published in *Le Rire* and has been anthologised by Carrière).

At first sight, Mirbeau may seem remote from this sort of humour, since his anti-colonialist opinions are fairly manifest. But black humour is always equivocal, and few writers entirely escape the prejudices of their age. Mirbeau favours a savagely ironical tone which is meant to subvert the racist discourse of colonialism from within (in the manner of Swift or Montesquieu in their famous apologias for cannibalism or slavery). In the discussion of cannibalism in *Le Jardin des supplices*, we learn that 'le nègre n'est pas comestible' and that it is preferable to eat Germans, 'plus gras que les autres races [...] Et puis [...] c'est un Allemand de moins!' (115). Killing negroes is essential, rather, 'pour les civiliser' (117). The theme recurs in *Les 21 Jours d'un neurasthénique* in the imaginary interview with General Archinard. This 'grand civilisateur soudanais' (112) has solved the problem of negroes' inedibility by using their hides to paper his study walls. 'Employés de cette façon, les nègres ne seront plus de la matière inerte, et nos colonies serviront du moins à quelque chose ...' (113). This method of securing a return on human flesh is no doubt a demonstration through the absurd — but what exactly is being demonstrated? That the civilising mission of colonialism is no more than a system of cynical exploitation? While the ostensible goal of colonialism is to impose the law on savage countries, in Mirbeau's opinion all laws are basically homicidal, sublimating 'la passion du meurtre', a destructive (but vital) instinct which he perceives as the foundation of Western society. However, Mirbeau tends to be ensnared in his own logic: if man is at bottom a murderous beast — a predatory carnivore like so many competing species in the animal kingdom — the exploitation of the weak by the strong would seem to be entirely justifiable, according to a crude notion of 'natural' law. In his conception of evil, Mirbeau seems to be caught between Sade and Rousseau: does evil derive from man, society or nature? In any case, is not human society an extension of nature, a natural phenomenon? Man is natural, and thus abominable (as Baudelaire said of woman). Consequently, to revolt against the order of things seems pointless, unless in fact one has a less pessimistic view of society and human nature.

Mirbeau's fascination with cruelty and exploitation does not betray a sadistic nihilism, but a more confused urge to revolt against the constrictions of established systems and orders; hence the rather sentimental anarchism with which he replaced his original affiliation to the reactionary right as he became more independent as a writer in the mid-1880s (Tolstoy supplanting a political dictator as a more respectable model). For all the gory fantasies which fill a book like *Le Jardin des supplices*, he saw himself (and was seen by some of his contemporaries) as a humanitarian writer whose mission was to expose and denounce the lies (or truths) which uphold the social order. The narrator of *Le 628–E8* insists on the pity he feels at human misfortune and his outrage at injustice (303). But as we shall see, on considering these texts in more detail, mystification and black humour invariably distort the satirical intent, so that complicity and delectation can easily replace indignation as the dominant tone.

Mirbeau himself called the revolutionary leaders of the Paris Commune 'bandits' and 'farceurs', just as he labelled pre-Raphaelite painters 'd'insupportables farceurs' and 'd'assez mornes fumistes' (cited by

Schwarz, 1971: 103 and by Nivet & Michel, 1990: 514). Returning the compliment, Edmond de Goncourt judged Mirbeau's libertarian ideology to be little better than a spurious joke, since it was so blatantly at odds with his opulent personal existence (*Journal*, 6 May 1892; III, 702–03). As Grojnowski and Sarrazin observe in their anthology of fin-de-siècle humour, *L'Esprit fumiste*, the humorist 'échappe aux autorités, au public, à lui-même, à Dieu' (1990: 36). Humour grants the writer a somewhat equivocal freedom, however perversely irresponsible it may sometimes appear. To conclude this discussion, we need to return from these remarks on the political or philosophical implications of the writer's sadistic vision to a more detailed analysis of Mirbeau's comic technique in practice, and particularly to his favourite device, caricature.

* * *

Caricature is commonly defined as a form of graphic (or verbal) representation whose most striking feature is the exaggeration of certain details of the subject depicted to create a humorous or mocking effect. Distortion and derision are essential elements. The caricature is an ideogram, which obliges the spectator (who in effect becomes a reader, as Baudelaire noted) to make a connection between the image and the model or type which it supposedly represents. For the reader chronologically or culturally removed from a particular caricature, the link and satirical message may be far from obvious; this is why many nineteenth-century drawings and jokes now seem to be impenetrable riddles, to be at best laboriously decoded. Yet as Baudelaire also argued (1968: 383), the ephemeral quality of certain images enhances their strangeness, lending them a 'réalité fantastique et saisissante' with the passage of time, a mythic quality which may rival the historical reality of the original model. Thus Philipon's celebrated series of pears is as memorable as the monarch Louis-Philippe whose metamorphosis from man to fruit was pictured in *Le Charivari* in 1834.

The caricatural code depends on reduction and simplification, an emblematic reification (Louis-Philippe as pear, Churchill as cigar). This is analogous to the evolutionary reductivism of certain nineteenth-century anthropologists who presented the negro as a near relative of the great apes. Nowadays, we are likely to interpret the series of anthropomorphic heads which show the stages of human evolution from monkey to man, with the black as an intermediate development, as closer to the fancies of a graphic artist like Grandville than to scientific research (Stephen Jay Gould's *The Mismeasure of Man* offers some memorable illustrations). Caricature often refers to an implicit typology in fact (race, class, gender, profession). Its reductivism is not necessarily a limitation; sometimes, this reveals an extraordinary inventiveness (Arcimboldo's famous composite heads are a good example).

Mirbeau's paradoxical status as a writer is further illustrated by his practice of caricature. Just as he was an anarchist *rentier* and anti-Semitic *dreyfusard*, so too he was a reluctant caricaturist. Unlike Baudelaire or Huysmans, who defended and analysed caricature, Mirbeau affected to detest what a contemporary critic called 'ce genre toujours un peu suspect et inquiétant' (Fournel, 1884: 496). While excluding an inspired artist like Daumier, Mirbeau confessed

> [n'avoir] pour la caricature en général et sa verve parodiste qu'une médiocre estime [...] Ses procédés de grossissement hideux et de déformation burlesque montrent trop l'impuissance et l'infériorité de ce métier, qui, ainsi compris, n'arrive jamais à la représentation ironique d'un type, à la synthèse satirique d'un événement, ce qui pourtant devrait être son seul but. [...] la caricature proprement dite est forcément bornée; on a vite franchi le champ de son action. Quand elle a grossi un nez, allongé des moustaches, donné aux ventres l'aspect d'une tonne, elle a tout dit.
>
> (*Combats esthétiques*, I, 214–15)

In sum, 'La caricature est une manifestation stérile de l'esprit' (216). This article, published in *La France* on 22 September 1885, is the only critical study Mirbeau devoted to the genre. The ill-tempered tone of his remarks suggests both a disenchanted idealism and a fairly reactionary perspective; the hierarchy of values implied by this diatribe reduces caricature to a minor, somewhat ignoble craft. Not only does it debase the human spirit, but it appeals to a general public which enjoys only the grossest spectacles such as vaudeville. Hence (in Mirbeau's jaundiced view) the success of mediocre draughtsmen like Cham, with his 'personnages qui ne tiennent d'aucune anatomie, d'aucun temps, d'aucun milieu social, qui ne sont ni des bêtes, ni des hommes, ni quoi que ce soit' (214). It should be recalled that in spite of his reputation as the champion of Monet and Rodin, Mirbeau did not always reveal progressive tastes when writing about art. On the contrary, he described the work of Matisse as a 'pauvre folie' produced by a 'paralytique général' (*Correspondance avec Monet*, 224), and derided the perverse transformations which art nouveau inflicted on everyday objects. Mirbeau has no hesitation in using caricature to denounce the caricatural vision of other artists, without apparently noticing the paradox that he is thereby employing the very form which he is attacking. To ridicule the excesses of 'Modern-style', the writer dreams up a fantastical coffee pot, 'en bouse de vache galvanisée [qui] représente ... un fromage de Roquefort' (*Combats esthétiques*, II, 309–10), for in this topsy-turvy universe, 'Tout tourne, se bistourne, se chantourne, se maltourne; tout roule, s'enroule, se déroule, et brusquement s'écroule' (*La 628-E8*, 320).

Henry James observed that 'it is evidently of the essence of caricature to be reactionary' (1954: 4). The caricaturist's starting point is inevitably a negative one, for his aim is to express his hatred or contempt for the subject he is depicting. Parodying the exaggerated mannerisms of art nouveau, Mirbeau displays an amusing verbal and phonetic inventiveness but also betrays his own aesthetic limitations. However, this misoneism (which he detested in others) is not enough to explain the apparent contradiction of a writer attacking a genre which he practises himself. Doubtless one could infer, somewhat unkindly, that when he denounces the sterility of caricature, the author is unconsciously acknowledging his own shortcomings as a literary creator; for Mirbeau, exaggeration and the burlesque are second nature. Nonetheless, he also perceives the possibility of a less circumscribed type of caricature, capable of creating universal types and crystalising events in a satirical synthesis. If Cham is condemned for ignoring reality, this new version of caricature is grounded in the real world but offers a comic, mythified vision of it.

Mirbeau refuses to be tied down by theories, preferring to claim contradiction and mystification as his guiding principles. Following the example of the surreal coffee pot, he persuades an ingenuous collector that a little stone jug which he picked up at a fair in Dijon is 'une des plus anciennes poteries coréennnes qui soient au monde' (*Combats esthétiques*, II, 425), in order to deride the credulity of art lovers who are unable to transform the ordinary into the extraordinary. Similarly, he contemptuously rejects the label art critic, 'cet animal pontifiant et parasitaire qui, le doigt levé, comme un apôtre, et la bouche torse par l'envie, comme un castrat, va raisonnant sur des choses qu'il ignore ou qu'il ne comprend pas!' (*Combats esthétiques*, II, 8). Mirbeau views himself as a 'simple promeneur', although his promenades in the world of art occupy more than a thousand pages in Michel and Nivet's recent edition. In an article entitled 'Palinodies!' (*L'Aurore*, 15 November 1898), he jubilantly asserts that 'j'ai donné, je l'avoue, le plus déplorable exemple d'inconsistance qui se puisse voir. [...] C'est mon droit, je pense, et c'est mon honneur; et c'est aussi la seule certitude par quoi je sente réellement que je suis resté d'accord avec moi-même' (*Combats politiques*, 203–04).

Caricature thus fits into Mirbeau's mystifying strategy and his efforts to subvert the establishment. As he observes in 'Palinodies!', certain targets are constants; despite the twists and turns of his moods and political allegiances, he always strove to break 'ces terribles chaînes de l'éducation, de la famille, des prêtres ou de l'Etat' (*Combats politiques*, 204), without ever really becoming a revolutionary or even a man of the left ('Au fond du révolté que je suis, il y a un réactionnaire timide qui sommeille': 'Propos belges', *Les Ecrivains*, I, 188). In May 1902, Mirbeau composed the entire text of one issue of the satirical weekly, *L'Assiette au beurre*. The 'têtes de Turc' assailed by Mirbeau and this journal were always close; appropriately, the priest and soldier pictured strangling a boy on the covers of recent editions of *Sébastien Roch* and *Contes cruels* (volume two) come from an illustration originally published in *L'Assiette au beurre*. The list of ideological adversaries obviously includes the judge, politician, coloniser and bloated bourgeois, but also those artists and intellectuals whom the author considers to be traitors to his notion of truth and nature. While Mirbeau's onslaughts on the rigid traditionalism of academic painting are hardly surprising, his mockery of the affected mannerism of pre-Raphaelite painters and their epigons indicates the parameters of his avant-gardism.

At the centre of Mirbeau's caricatural technique we find the physiognomical portrait in the tradition of La Bruyère. In other words, the physical normally expresses the moral, which corresponds to Judith Wechsler's definition of caricature as 'a visual commentary on its time whose vehicle [is] the human figure' (1982: 68). The literary portrait can be visual only in a metaphorical sense, evidently, but written representation of the human form in Mirbeau's work is highly concrete and frequently grotesque. His characters tend to fit into three categories. First, the protagonist or the narrator in many novels and stories is often an autobiographical projection whose relative psychological density falls outside the scope of this analysis. On the other hand, the majority of secondary characters in Mirbeau's fiction tend to be shells or puppets whose existence rarely extends beyond the flabby flesh or ludicrous gestures which capture and define them. The reifying hyperbole which the writer so enjoys allows for easy identification of the innumerable members of this large family. A mincing youth is 'beau comme une femme, souple comme un gant, mince et blond comme un cigare'; a repulsive servant woman has lips which hang down 'comme la margelle usée d'un vieux puits'; the soul of Captain Mauger, a 'grotesque et sinistre fantoche', is impenetrable for 'le néant' and 'le vide' are unknowable (*Le Journal d'une femme de chambre*, 206, 290, 282). Likewise, Sébastien Roch's father may well possess a stomach which seems 'énorme et menaçant, sous le tablier de cotonnade', but 'la solennité bouffonne de ses gestes' and his worn hat give him 'l'air d'une caricature ancienne' (*Sébastien Roch*, 61, 237). As for the third category, these are contemporary personalities who are presented either directly or under a thin disguise, usually in parodic or derisory fashion, so that they become caricatures of themselves. Mirbeau liked writing articles consisting of a fabricated interview with a well-known public figure whose absurd utterances speak for themselves. This use of imitation is really nearer to parody than caricature.

In presenting his teratological gallery, Mirbeau makes use of anthropomorphism or zoomorphism, as well as the extravagant metaphors which have already been mentioned. His aim is to strike the reader's imagination, by offering a burlesque image whose immediacy has a graphic effect, even if the verisimilitude or coherence of the narrative are put at risk. He reveals a pre-Sartrian fascination with viscosity and liquefaction, as well as an urge to reduce the human face to a grimacing mask. If the mask symbolises a reified humanity, a grotesque object stripped of essence, it also has a totemic value, as a sort of hypnotic Gorgon's head (Claude Herzfeld has written a suggestive, albeit cryptic essay on this theme). The mask embodies a condition which is degraded but also compelling. Mirbeau's early career in 1883 included the editorship of a Bonapartist journal called *Les Grimaces*, where he indulged his apocalyptic fervour by calling down cholera or a dictator on his decomposing, decadent compatriots, just as the previous year he had railed against their seduction by the 'impudentes fatuités' of the actor, a 'roi absolu' with 'sa face grimée et flétrie par le fard' (*Combats politiques*, 44). In a sense, by taking up literary caricature, Mirbeau has embraced the grimaces which mark the success of the actor, both rival and model for the writer.

In this universe bound to damnation or decomposition, appearance replaces or becomes essence. The 'masque inspiré' of the abbé Jules finally ceases to cover 'le ricanement du mystificateur', for the character does not exist apart from his mystifications. This 'masque verdâtre et maigre' is the physiognomical correlative of the 'déformation de la nature' which forms the basis of religion and the social order (*L'Abbé Jules*, 130, 169, 146). The summary code of behaviour and human relations established in Mirbeau's fiction thus obeys a principle of distortion which is universal as much as aesthetic. Pierre Gobin has stressed the importance of posture in Mirbeau's works: the opposition and repetition of gestures and parts of the body reflect an obvious symbolic intent. Whereas for instance 'les riches sont des ventres, les pauvres sont [...] des dos. [...] Le dos brisé est l'expression muette de la douleur morale et de l'aliénation sociale' (1975: 202). So in *Le Calvaire* we observe Breton fishermen, 'ces brutes magnifiques avec leurs mains calleuses, leurs yeux tout pleins d'infini, et leurs dos qui font pleurer' (242).

This gesticulatory or carnal code is of course found in many authors. In the context of fin-de-siècle fiction, we recall the struggle of the fat and the thin in Zola's *Le Ventre de Paris* (1873), and more generally the symbolic display of battered, bloated or malnourished flesh which typifies so many of the naturalist novels following this model. The fact remains that Mirbeau's tireless inventory of physiological and psychological tics and traits does create a corporeal typology whose comic originality cannot be denied. When it comes to chopping up bodies, Mirbeau combines nausea and black humour with a grotesque verve akin to Sade or Huysmans, as the study of some choice morsels reveals.

The narrator of 'Piédanat' paints the portrait of a disgusting old procuress:

> Sa main surtout attirait mon attention, une main courte et grasse, creusée de fossettes profondes, dont les doigts semblaient de caoutchouc, une patte répugnante de bête visqueuse qui paraissait faite exprès pour tripoter de sales choses.   (*Contes cruels*, II, 35)

In Mirbeau's physiognomic system, the smallest detail or part of the body can signify the vicious nature of the whole person. In fact, the individual is reduced to such fragments, which acquire an autonomous existence through metaphor: the fingers are at once reified, animalised and liquefied (flesh becomes rubber, solid viscous, the hand a paw). The writer inflicts a process of dissolution upon the human body, a satirical, fantastical transformation.

Célestine, the eponymous narrator of *Le Journal d'une femme de chambre*, elaborates a theory of physiognomy towards the end of her story, in the manner of Balzac or Proust. Surreptitiously observing an old lady who is interrogating a fearful servant, she is at first astonished not to behold 'un nez crochu, de longues dents dépassant la lèvre, un œ il jaune et rond d'épervier'. But this stereotypical image of the mistress as tyrannical witch would not suffice to express the fundamental malevolence of the character in question. One needs to go beyond outer appearances to achieve a more sophisticated, less literal analysis, for former shopkeepers of this sort 'ont ce talent de se composer des physionomies spéciales, où rien ne transparaît de leur nature intérieure'. Just as in Proust the displaced snobbery of Legrandin is finally betrayed by the servile curve of his fleshy posterior, so too Mirbeau's observer probes 'les intimités de l'être, ou [...] des surfaces corporelles, ordinairement dépourvues de tout caractère expressif', in order to reveal 'les instincts bas, les ambitions féroces'. In this case, the gaze returns to the fingers, 'pareils à des serres, sur une proie vivante', to the hostile back, but above all to the back of the neck: 'Sa nuque était son vrai visage, et ce visage était terrible' (*Le Journal d'une femme de chambre*, 317–19).

As this phrase with its echoes of Balzac shows, Mirbeau enjoys decoding the subtle movements of physiognomy, although the operation always remains on the surface. He also likes playing octaves on the scale of evolution. Seeing characters as animals is a common device: a judge 'ressemblait à un singe' (*L'Abbé Jules*, 47); as for a sacristan, 'crâne aplati, peau fripée, jaunâtre et grenue, il ressemblait à un crapaud' and needless to say displays 'toutes les manières visqueuses et rampantes des cloportes ecclésiastiques' (*Le Journal d'une femme de chambre*, 195, 336). It goes without saying that in Mirbeau's lexicon, the word 'ecclésiastique' and its synonyms have a pejorative meaning. Nevertheless, his zoomorphism is not simply degrading and regressive. As we shall see, in *Le Journal d'une femme de chambre*, the character Joseph is transformed from a subhuman status to become a supernatural predator. Indeed, the author likes animals as much as or more than mankind. Writing as a fabulist, he turns animals into men. In households which practise unnatural vice, a dog can have 'des passions comme un homme'; this beast would even be preferable as a lover to the egregious Captain Mauger (*Le Journal d'une femme de chambre*, 225, 277). Animals emulate men, and men animals. The thesis is explored further in *La 628–E8* and *Dingo*, although in these later works, Mirbeau abandons the caricatural snapshot for a more sustained type of allegory.

We can conclude this discussion by noting that the writer's caricatural vision essentially turns the abnormal into a new norm. His characters are cast in a grotesque but predictable mould. Mirbeau sought to justify this aesthetic on the grounds that

> ordinairement, je ne me refuse pas à accepter pour vraies les choses les plus invraisemblables, lesquelles sont, en général, toujours en dessous de la réalité, car, plus je vais dans la vie, et plus je m'aperçois que c'est la vie qui exagère, et non ceux qui sont chargés de l'exprimer.
>
> (*Combats esthétiques*, II, 325)

Any great artist must confront this deadly, elusive reality. Praising Van Gogh, Mirbeau highlights his marvellous ability to embody 'les aspects féeriques de la nature, la joie énorme et magnifique, la fête miraculeuse de la vie' (*Combats esthétiques*, II, 297). Such spontaneous, overflowing lyricism is remote from the stylised simplification of caricature. To resort to caricature is thus to accept second best, however expressive may be the mythic 'idiom of terrifying masks' (Gombrich, 1977: 301) which Mirbeau succeeded in devising. This confrontation with a nature both enchanted and accursed is the subject of *Le Jardin des supplices*, to which we now turn.

Chapter Three
Petals of Blood

> De même qu'autrefois nous partions pour la
> Chine... (Baudelaire, 'Le Voyage')

Le Jardin des supplices is a disturbing and provocative book, likely to give a guilty conscience to anyone who opts to explore the crimson, verdant pages of this strange horticultural torture catalogue, for the reader becomes an involuntary accomplice in the atrocity exhibition concocted by Mirbeau's algolagnic imagination. This 'Bible du sadisme', as the libertarian poet Laurent Tailhade called it (*Le Jardin des supplices*, 309), was published in June 1899; poised at the century's end, looking back to the fantasies of evil invented by the Marquis de Sade as he languished in the prisons of the Ancien Régime, and looking forward to the grimmer reality of parodic justice and mass extermination practised by the totalitarian states of our own century. An obvious literary predecessor was that other 'Bible of decadence', Huysmans' *A rebours*, published fifteen years earlier, complete with a nightmarish chapter on hothouse blooms; while as a satirical, ambiguous exploration of the colonialist venture and its excesses, Conrad's long novella *Heart of Darkness* forms a strikingly similar English counterpart (published only two months before Mirbeau's novel).

Mirbeau is remembered as the author of *Le Jardin des supplices* precisely because of the excessiveness of its subject: that is, a reflection on the aesthetics of torture, illustrated with practical demonstrations. The two principal characters (an anonymous first-person narrator and his English mistress Clara) are sent off to China to discover the obscene dystopia which illustrates the theme. To this geographical distancing is added Mirbeau's habitual oblique mode of narration: the story is told retrospectively by the protagonist on his return to Europe, the text of the novel consisting of the manuscript which he reads out to a gathering of Parisian intellectuals and sophisticates. The presence of this group is established in an extended preamble recounted by a separate, equally unidentified narrator; needless to say, women, workers or foreigners are excluded from the group, which does not reappear after this prologue. A third factor which further dilutes the virulence of the book is the fact that Mirbeau's Orientalism is entirely literary, if not second hand. He never set foot outside Europe, although this did not deter him from publishing a series of 'Lettres sur l'Inde' attributed to a pseudonymous traveller (though actually based on the first-hand knowledge of the diplomat François Deloncle) in *Le Gaulois* and *Le Journal des débats* in 1885 (reprinted by Michel and Nivet as *Lettres de l'Inde*, 1991). While such features cumulatively tend to push us towards an allegorical reading of the book (as a parable on colonialism, justice, love and death, individual rights, the vegetable kingdom), the uncomfortable fact remains that what most impresses and repels are the ghastly authenticity and naturalistic morbidity realism of *Le Jardin des supplices*.

In the first instance, I would prefer to look at Mirbeau's presentation of his characters' quest within the Chinese garden, and its strange blending of animal, vegetable and mineral, before returning to questions of narrative form and the satirical treatment of Western imperialism. Critical accounts of the book (such as the articles published in the *Cahiers Octave Mirbeau* or proceedings of the Angers conference, entitled *Octave Mirbeau*), while opening up fruitful lines of investigation, usually hold its atrocities at bay by enveloping them in the austere, somewhat opaque tones of academic discourse. It is indeed difficult to steer a safe course between undue censoriousness, prudishness or prurience. Admittedly, it is hard to imagine anyone nowadays reading such an eminently literary work for more than scholarly gratification. We watch Clara and her pusillanimous lover watching spectacles of violent horror, but are unlikely to share their delectation. The repetition and accumulation of horror in any case attenuate its intensity and ultimately become monotonous or grotesquely comic. Finally, after our extended tour round this garden fertilised by the corpses of 30,000 coolies, we cease to be surprised at beholding yet another victim of ever more ingenious torture staked out among the birds and flowers. These are victims moreover of a system of justice whose functionings remain remote and arbitrary. Towards the end of the novel, Clara and the narrator walk beneath trees from which are suspended like overgrown bunches of fruit the tortured bodies of prisoners on remand, whose guilt of any crime seems anything but certain; such as the woman whose eyelids, nostrils, lips and genitals have been rubbed with red pepper and whose nipples are crushed between two metal nuts (244). This seemingly gratuitous spectacle is also observed by a gathering of vultures and ravens, as well as the informers hoping to harvest a confession from the mouths of the crucified detainees. The punishment thus precedes the crime. The aleatory gratuitousness of such episodes may strike Clara as erotically exciting, but the reader is more probably meant to attend to the fundamental immorality of the torture garden, where the dubious equilibrium between crime and punishment found in Western systems of justice (where individuals are supposed to enjoy certain rights) is dispensed with and replaced by exercises in sadistic aestheticism. However, unlike the philosophical libertines of Sade's *Les 120 Journées de Sodome* or *La Philosophie dans le boudoir*, Mirbeau's protagonists are not active agents of destruction; neither are they themselves sacrificed to the destructive mechanism, in the fashion of Kafka's central figures in 'In the Penal Colony' or *The Trial*. Nor yet do they embrace the heart of darkness like Conrad's Kurtz, who becomes himself a false idol, a 'pitiful Jupiter' and finally succumbs to 'The horror! The horror!' (*Heart of Darkness*, 224, 239). Rather they remain disengaged contemplators or voyeurs who penetrate the enclosed space of the garden for a few hours, mainly to awaken jaded appetites. For Clara, this appears to be a regular outing to fill up a boring Wednesday (her nervous breakdown comes afterwards); while the narrator trails along, fulfilling the final part of the 'mission' which brought him to the East, in a derisory voyage of initiation.

Michel Delon, the editor of Gallimard's 'Folio' version of the text, argues that Mirbeau 'fait de la Chine en même temps l'antithèse et la métaphore de l'Europe' and that consequently '*Le Jardin des supplices* constitue peut-être l'équivalent, pour la Belle Epoque, des *Lettres persanes*' (for the regency of Louis XV) (17, 18). Montesquieu's Persia or Mirbeau's China, in other words, are both alien, essentially other, but also purely literary creations which act as a satirical mirror for Western society. Another, more obvious parallel in the eighteenth century is Voltaire's *Candide*. Just as Voltaire's book parodies the conventions of the exotic adventure novel in order to reflect on social or metaphysical evil, so too Mirbeau portrays an ingenuous, albeit corruptible hero who passes alongside suffering and catastrophe while remaining personally unscathed, until he arrives in the infernal paradise of the garden which devours and annihilates those sent to cultivate it. But whereas Voltaire ends his tale with the famous injunction to work the garden in a spirit of collective enterprise, Mirbeau's protagonist remains trapped in a regressive cycle of frustrated desire.

So although they escape physical torture, Mirbeau's characters are certainly emotionally scarred by their experience of the garden. The narrator appears in the prologue as 'un homme, à la figure ravagée, le dos voûté' (57). His deliberate anonymity ('Peu importe mon nom!' (63)) clearly marks his loss of social and personal identity. If he is a failed politician and explorer, his partner, the enigmatic Clara, supposedly embodies 'à elle seule toute la nature!' (61), a weighty responsibility indeed. Unsurprisingly, she often seems weighed down by fin-de-siècle stereotypes of feminine vice, suggested immediately by her red hair, green eyes and Englishness (curiously, in French nineteenth-century fiction, the English tend to represent either bumbling imbecility — like the entomologist Sir Oscar Terwick who features briefly at the end of part two of *Le Jardin des supplices* — or total depravity). But typically, Clara's libertinism proves to be a curse rather than a perverted form of liberty; this 'fée des charniers' is the victim of her sadomasochistic obsession, an 'âme éperdue et folle' (228, 217).

The lacerating materialism of Mirbeau's descriptions is in fact remote from the sprightly ironies of either Voltaire or Montesquieu. *Le Jardin des supplices* is a lushly sensual book, where the initial impression of well-documented naturalism finally gives way to a fantastical hyper-realism. The sarcastic tone of the first two parts, the 'Frontispice' and 'En mission', is rather different from the agonised lyrical outpourings which increasingly invade the pages of the third, longest section entitled 'Le Jardin des supplices'. This final part marks the characters' arrival in China, after their previous voyage from Marseille to Ceylon, although there is an odd chronological hiatus at this point: we learn that the narrator abandoned Clara in Canton to spend two years travelling in Annam on another self-imposed 'mission', but has now returned to her thraldom in an unnamed 'ville maudite et sublime' in the South (151–52). Evil and suffering at once invade this existence, and needless to say manifest themselves in the most repellent physical, physiological forms. In the opening chapter of 'Le Jardin des supplices', the narrator learns of the death of Clara's female companion, Annie (whom he effectively replaces), 'de cette lèpre effrayante qu'on appelle l'éléphantiasis'. The victim undergoes a bizarre metamorphosis into a sort of vegetable:

> Sa peau, plus rose et d'une plus fine pulpe que la fleur de l'althœ a, se durcit, s'épaissit, s'enfla, devint d'un gris cendreux ... de grosses tumeurs, de monstrueux tubercules la soulevèrent. [...] Oh! son visage, son visage! ... Figurez-vous une poche énorme, une outre ignoble, toute grise, striée de sang brun ... et qui pendait et qui se balançait au moindre mouvement de la malade ... (144)

And this sickness is so contagious that it affects the mineral kingdom: her very jewels are infected, 'les perles mouraient sur sa peau [...] en quelques jours, atteintes de la lèpre, elles se changeaient en de menues boules de cendre [...] Saviez-vous qu'il y eût des âmes dans les perles?' This incidental detail Clara finds 'affolant et délicieux' (146); whereas, in a more predictable horrific coda, even the vultures spurn the dead woman's body, which has to be burned.

Such episodes seemingly break the conventions of naturalistic realism which the documentary novel usually follows, encouraging us to read Mirbeau's text as a morbid fairy story, where fears rather than wishes are fulfilled through partly supernatural means. (Although, as Larousse's *Grand Dictionnaire universel du XIXe siècle* reminds us, pearls themselves are 'le résultat d'un accident morbide dans la sécrétion de la matière nacrée' in the oyster's shell, and can easily deteriorate 'par l'usage, le frottement, les acides ou même la simple transpiration'.) Annie took poison to escape her deliquescent flesh, and Clara imagines for her a second, less hideous transformation in the shape of the little pink cloud which appears at the same time each day above the garden, like 'une petite barque, avec des voiles de soie' (230). This fancy allows the self freed from its corrupt carnality to achieve a sort of vaporous transcendence, but the metamorphosis is effected through a grim agony and loss of individual consciousness.

The narrator of *Dans le ciel* suffers an attack of meningitis, an illness which 'avait en quelque sorte liquéfié mon cerveau' (45). This however he finds to be a state of happiness and regrets that he survives the experience, a good indication of how individual consciousness can be perceived as a curse, just as the apparent solidity of the body is purely deceptive. A metaphor repeated obsessively in *Le Jardin des supplices* describes the body as 'ce petit tas de fumier, cette menue pincée de pourriture' (55). Fertiliser is a useful enough product, but the narrator prefers to connect physical to moral corruption, and laments 'ce crime: l'univers' (47), excused only by beauty. The garden with its cycle of propagation and destruction stands for this universe (248–50), although the notion of criminality seems to imply the existence of laws whose existence is paradoxically denied at the same time.

There is in fact an apparent contrast between the narrator, constrained by the remnants of a timorous Christianity (he sententiously requests his listeners to wish peace 'aux cendres de son péché' (63)) and Clara who appeals to 'la resplendissante et divine immoralité des choses' (225). Yet in practice she is as much the prisoner of her warped desire as the prisoners tortured under the great bell in the garden (266). No organic being escapes the destructive principle built into the life cycle, those with consciousness suffering most in the process. *Le Jardin des supplices* does indeed suggest that vegetables may be better off than animals in the scheme of things. Certainly, the former may devour the latter, contrary to usual expectations. The flies which gorge themselves on human remains are themselves devoured by those notorious plants whose spathes obscenely mimic human organs:

> à l'extérieur d'un jaune verdâtre de décomposition, et semblables à des thorax ouverts de bêtes mortes... Du fond de ces cornets, sortaient de longs spadices sanguinolents, imitant la forme de monstrueux phallus ... (224)

Mirbeau's rival Paul Bourget was one of the first commentators to characterise the literature of decadence in his *Essais de psychologie contemporaine* (1883 and 1899) as marked by the dissolution of thematic and rhetorical forms and haunted by myths of degeneration and regeneration. Unsurprisingly, examples abound in Mirbeau's novel. Both the abject bourgeois frightened to death in a train compartment by the homicidal son of one Dr Trépan and the sinister cackling executioner in the garden are endowed with a characteristic gross belly which 'tremblait et roulait ainsi qu'un ignoble paquet de gélatine' (55, cf. 204). While this simile dissolves the body in a fairly conventional caricatural twist, the executioner practises a more radical sculptural butchery, redesigning the bodies of his victims and changing their sexes when the mood takes him. Further images relating to decomposition and primeval slime recur throughout the book (much as they do in *Heart of Darkness*). The 'intolérable odeur' of mud clings to the corrupt politician Eugène Mortain, who likewise seeks to plunge his reluctant associate, the narrator, into the slimy void (84, 90). On the other hand, Clara's chaste friendship on board the *Saghalien* transforms this soiled past 'en lumineux azur' and displays 'l'avenir à travers la tranquille, la limpide émeraude des bonheurs réguliers' (111). The metaphor turns what is tainted and organic into something mineral and durable, just as a woman's breasts in the poem 'Les Trois Amies' are as firm and rounded as 'une couple de vases d'or' (177 and 230). The jewel generally escapes contamination. Thus seen through a fine spray of water, 'dans laquelle se jouaient toutes les couleurs de l'arc-en-ciel, [...] les gazons et les fleurs prenaient des translucidités de pierres précieuses' (186). The crimson leaves of an immense ash tree 'donnaient l'illusion d'un dôme de rubis' (187). But the perception is indeed optative and illusory: the poem turns in conclusion to the third woman, whose breasts and belly 'exhalent l'odeur du poisson', which makes her most attractive of all, for she conveys 'La pourriture en qui réside la chaleur éternelle de la vie, / En qui s'élabore l'éternel renouvellement des métamorphoses!' (177 and 230).

This ambivalent paean to the infinitely variable dissolution of forms is further illustrated by one of Sade's libertines, who explains that murder is a purely relative notion:

> le pouvoir de détruire n'est pas accordé à l'homme, il a tout au plus celui de varier des formes, mais il n'a pas celui de les anéantir; or toute forme est égale aux yeux de la nature, rien ne se perd dans le creuset immense où ses variations s'exécutent.   (*Les Infortunes de la vertu*, 66)

In this context, it is worth recalling that Mirbeau adopted the pseudonym 'Nirvana' when he wrote some of his *Lettres de l'Inde* fourteen years before *Le Jardin des supplices*, suggesting thereby the mystical urge to extinguish desire and be embraced by the world spirit. However, his fictional heroes as a rule prefer impotent indignation to serene resignation and mystification to mysticism. The narrator's struggle with the vegetable kingdom in *Le Jardin des supplices* finally amounts to a failure to embrace otherness, a yearning revealed by the writer himself. Writing to Monet, Mirbeau grumbles about the perversity of his flowers (which shrink when they should be growing) and the futility of literature, 'engluée dans ses erreurs métaphysiques, abrutie par la fausse poésie du panthéisme idiot et barbare'; one would do better to interrogate the infinity of space, or to 'chercher, au fond des mers primitives, la mucosité primordiale, d'où nous venons' (*Correspondance avec Monet*, 102–03). In truth

> Il n'y a que la terre. Moi, j'en arrive à trouver une motte de terre admirable et je reste des heures entières en contemplation devant elle. Et le terreau! J'aime le terreau comme on aime une femme. Je m'en barbouille et je vois dans les tas fumants les belles formes et les belles couleurs qui naîtront de là! (111)

When he comes across a fine supply of manure, 'comme on n'en trouve plus', he hastens to *butter* the garden with it (112).

Decomposing matter may suit the gardener, but Mirbeau's fictional protagonist enjoys a more derisory, ambiguous relationship with the vegetable kingdom from the beginning of his existence. His father was a grain merchant, who specialised in adulterating his produce with water, gravel or poisonous seeds and finally managed to ruin himself by poisoning a whole barracks. The son, as we have seen, subsequently stood for parliament as a 'candidat betteravier', but despite this vegetable's importance in the rural economy was outmatched by a more devious rival. The narrator is adopted by his former schoolmate Mortain as his 'homme de paille' (83) and eventually given a spurious mission as an embryologist to seek out the primordial life cell in Ceylon. An alternative mission would have taken him to Oceania in order to 'étudier les divers systèmes d'administration pénitentiaire qui y fonctionnent' (97) and their wider relevance to France.

All this, we learn, is but an 'immense blague' (98), perpetrated by 'un mystificateur qui s'amuse à se mystifier soi-même' (77). The irony is, of course, that he does eventually come close to fulfilling both missions, combining biological and penal investigation in the torture garden. Commenting belatedly on his derisory dismissal of the natural world, exemplified by his facile puns about palm trees (also compared to 'd'affreux et chauves plumeaux' (137–38)), the narrator regrets this blasphemy 'contre la beauté infinie de la Forme'(108). The second half of the book changes its tone rather surprisingly, cynical professions of ignorance being replaced by an apparently encyclopedic knowledge of botany, celebrated with a frenzied, hysterical lyricism. The reversal is supposedly effected through Clara, the erotic intermediary not only between Western and Oriental culture (and the narrator claims that love brought him poetic, descriptive skills (107)), but also between nature and culture; she herself is an 'Eve des paradis merveilleux, fleur elle-même, fleur d'ivresse, et fruit savoureux de l'éternel désir' (110).

The doctor who appears in the book's prologue reminds us, however, that woman is 'admirablement amphibologique' (60). So too is Mirbeau's treatment of floral imagery. Turning people into botanic forms may enhance their aesthetic appeal, but at the same time their humanity is obviously sacrificed. Mme G... , the society procuress, is 'un énorme paquet de fleurs roulantes, de plumes dansantes, de dentelles déferlantes', who 'ne pouvant plus cultiver la fleur du vice en son propre jardin, la cultivait en celui des autres' (85, 87). Likewise, the faces of the women waiting before the prison gates are 'comme une poussée de fleurs immenses, comme un tournoiement d'oiseaux féeriques' (167). Rather like the compost heaps in the garden fed by a daily supply of corpses, Mirbeau's text turns human humous into a variegated, bizarre flora.

* * *

The dissolution of forms in a biological or rhetorical sense also connects to Mirbeau's treatment of social and political corruption, as well his use or abuse of the conventions of literary fiction. Unsurprisingly, the prolix executioner complains to Clara that 'Il y a en Chine, milady, quelque chose de pourri' (205), referring not to the malodorous remains of his victims, but rather to a decadent political system, where under the nefarious influence of the West, technology and bureaucracy have replaced the long-standing tradition of individual artistry in torture. Jennifer Birkett characterises *Le Jardin de supplices* as 'a bitter satire on decadence' (1986: 159). Mirbeau's active involvement in the campaign to exculpate Captain Dreyfus is often cited as a specific reason for his disillusioned attitude towards social justice or injustice in his two most notorious novels, *Le Jardin des supplices* and *Le Journal d'une femme de chambre*. Between the publication of the two books, of course, Dreyfus had been returned to France, retried in Rennes, and found guilty all over again in September 1899, to the dismay of his supporters. But while *Le Jardin des supplices* obviously ridicules some of the sadistic posturing of Western colonists (witness the grotesque characters who feature in chapters five and six of 'En mission'), the author ultimately seems to celebrate decadence as much as he subverts its excesses. Dorgelès's remark that Mirbeau with his 'anarchisme de salon' displays 'une mauvaise foi qui me ravit' (1952: 155, 130) comes closer to the ambiguous complicity of his writing and of our response to it.

Satire and celebration need not be mutually exclusive. Ronald Hayman sees the Marquis de Sade as both immoralist and comedian (1978: 198). In similar fashion, Mirbeau's biographers remind us that *Le Jardin des supplices* inspired innumerable jokes among the author's contemporaries. Having to watch Rostand's play *L'Aiglon* was a torture which Mirbeau had missed off his catalogue, said Paul Morand (cited by Nivet, 1987: 356). When Michel and Nivet call *Le Jardin des supplices* 'cette monstruosité littéraire' (1990: 610), they are referring not simply to its gruesome subject matter, but to the composition (or decomposition) of the book itself. There is no doubt that these two commentators have added considerably to our knowledge of the book's origins, in the form of twenty or so prepublications in journals between 1892 and 1898 (see Nivet, 1987: 334, 348 and the *Cahiers Octave Mirbeau*, 1994: 171–92). Such material certainly demonstrates the writer's skill in conflating diverse texts within a single book, or what Pierre Michel calls his 'désinvolture', 'son absolu refus de composer' (*Cahiers Mirbeau*, 1994: 174). But does such detailed knowledge of Mirbeau's journalistic work necessarily add to the appreciation of the final product, his books? It is perhaps difficult to avoid the temptation, when one approaches Mirbeau from this genetic perspective, to reduce the novels to a patchwork stitched up from all the pieces which the author found in his drawer.

It is true that there is an obvious disproportion between the three sections into which the novel is divided, in terms of setting, tone and length. The 'Frontispice' runs to twenty pages (9% of the text); part one, 'En mission' occupies seventy-nine pages (35% of the text); and part two, 'Le Jardin des supplices' 128 pages (56%). But this asymmetry surely reflects a deliberate progression and intensification of effects: the initial philosophical discussion in Paris is illustrated in practice, firstly by the voyage and biography which precedes it in part one, covering many years, and then more extensively by the protracted experience of the garden, compressed into a single day. This narrative pattern is not dissimilar to that of *Heart of Darkness*, with the difference that Conrad brings his protagonist Marlow back to the present of narration, whereas Mirbeau dispenses with any such epilogue.

We know that the 'Frontispice' originated in articles published in 1892 and 1896, called 'La Loi du meurtre' and 'Divagations sur le meurtre' (*Le Jardin des supplices*, 305). This prologue consists of a theoretical discussion on the function of instinct in humankind, written with grating humour. Before it comes an authorial dedication: 'Aux Prêtres, aux Soldats, aux Juges, aux Hommes, qui éduquent, dirigent, gouvernent les hommes, je dédie ces pages de Meurtre et de Sang', signed 'O.M.'. From the beginning, then, we are made aware that the book will combine provocation and sensationalism with discussion of social or anthropological issues. Having noted in 1898 that 'les foules ne sont pas sensibles à l'ironie' (*L'Affaire Dreyfus*, 85), doubtless the author preferred to aim his sarcastic dedication directly at those who hold social and political power. Unlike, say, Jules Vallès, who dedicated his fictionalised account of the Paris Commune of 1871, *L'Insurgé* (1885) to the 'victimes de l'injustice sociale', in order to create a solidarity of the oppressed, 'la grande fédération des douleurs', Mirbeau's target is those who uphold the established order, with their symbolic capital letter ('[les] Hommes qui gouvernent les hommes'): the priest in the sphere of religion and education (witness *Sébastien Roch*); the soldier who defends the nation; the judge charged with the execution of the law. Mirbeau's offering is obviously a poisoned chalice; these three figureheads, like those of Genet's play, *Le Balcon* (1956), are derisory and interchangeable incarnations of an order which, as they well know, is a synonym for disorder.

The Europeans who appear in *Le Jardin des supplices* are almost exclusively members of the ruling or colonising classes. Clara is the only major female figure; she also belongs to this class. We learn that she is twenty-eight, was born in Canton, and that her deceased father was an opium dealer; hence presumably her financial and moral independence. The nameless narrator, as aspiring and largely unsuccessful politician, lover and writer, has a more tenuous hold on social status. On the other hand, the majority of Asians who appear are either servants or anonymous victims of the torture garden (some of them are disgraced members of the wealthier classes, like the voiceless poet in the prison or the banker condemned to the torture of the bell). The novel's characters thus fall into two separate categories, which clearly reflect the racial divisions of a segregated, colonial society, where Europeans exploit native Chinese (the spectators who come to observe the prisoners' torments are European women).

The infamous 'jardin des supplices' itself is enclosed within the centre of a prison located in an unnamed city in Southern China. We are told that it was created during the eighteenth century over a period of twenty-two years. In other words, it predates the colonial incursions of Western powers, and its authority seems to derive from the imperial system of Chinese justice, whose higher functioning and functionaries remain shrouded in mystery; no judges or magistrates actually appear in the book. Similarly, the torturers who do feature in the story often prove to be as vulnerable as those they torture: thus we see the men who work the gigantic bell themselves dying of exhaustion, driven on by a merciless superior in a regressive hierarchy of torturers. Although the foreign concession areas in late nineteenth-century China were subject to 'mixed' courts, dominated by Western legal practices, the system of justice portrayed in *Le Jardin des supplices* manifestly belongs to a culture alien and barbaric to modern Western observers. Mirbeau's graphic account of torture recalls Foucault's celebrated description of the execution by quartering in 1757 of the would-be regicide Damiens, under the Ancien Régime, when physical punishment was still a popular spectacle and the criminal's body was inscribed with 'an art of unbearable sensations' (1977: 11). Late nineteenth-century China was, in the words of a contemporary historian, a curious amalgam of a semi-colonial state (dominated by Britain, France and Japan) and of a medieval polity, 'with the government and people forming separate entities' (Hsü, 1983: 343–44). Imperial law 'was primarily a prescription of punishments', with the degree of punishment matching the offender's status rather than the crime; torture was used to extract confessions, and judicial decapitation and 'lingering death' were abolished only in 1910 (Chen, 1973: 10, 41).

Such details suggest that Mirbeau's depiction of the terrors of Chinese justice is not grossly exaggerated, although neither the commentators cited above nor other reference works consulted offer any evidence that the torture garden actually existed as an institution. The author is much less interested in the historical reality of China than in offering concrete illustration for the theses elaborated in the prologue of his novel. At the beginning of the book, notaries (and women) are excluded from the discussion on homicide. Notaries, like lawyers or porters, symbolise 'un état moyen de la mentalité française' (43). Thus although the symposium deals specifically with human criminality and especially with the female variety, both those whose professional occupation is to interpret the law and those women who embody moral corruption are banned from contributing.

Although this closed circle is essential for the spontaneous expression of 'idées intimes' (44), it is remote from those enclosed, secret places where Sade's libertines gather to pursue their atrocious pleasures. In Mirbeau's works, the potent, Sadeian aristocrat has degenerated into an vacillating, uninspiring bourgeois. Moreover, the characters in the prologue of *Le Jardin des supplices* are no more than voices, whose words are mockingly recorded by a separate initial narrator; the story told by Clara's lover is embedded in this opening account. This mode of dual narration recalls that used by Maupassant in many stories, although the anecdote which triggers the main plot is obviously much extended. Sartre in fact claimed that Maupassant's exploitation of oblique narration 'constitue la technique de base pour tous les romanciers français de sa génération' (1978: 176) and perceived it as fundamentally dishonest. Social criticism becomes a mere pretence, in an account of 'un bref désordre qui s'est annulé, [...] racontée du point de vue de l'expérience et de la sagesse, [...] écoutée du point de vue de l'ordre', where the narrator is 'un professionnel de l'expérience' disengaged from his story (173–74).

The schema may oversimplify, but the fact remains that Mirbeau's worldly reunion in *Le Jardin des supplices* does contain elitist, egotistical elements which may strike a hostile reader as stupidly reactionary. For instance, it becomes clear that an individual, homicidal act is considered more significant than charity or solidarity; witness the space devoted to the murderous zeal of the young Trépan, who terrifies an unappealing fat man to death in a railway compartment (55–57), thereby anticipating the famous *acte gratuit* of Gide's Lafcadio in *Les Caves du Vatican* by fifteen years. Are the reflections on murder in this 'Frontispice' to be taken as profound truths or silly banalities? (Mirbeau offers both possibilities within the text (43–44), which indicates how a certain self-directed irony often helps him forestall potential criticism.) Taken seriously, his project is an ambitious one: like Freud, he is attempting to lay out a pessimistic, determinist theory of human behaviour, which accounts for good and evil, unconscious motivation, the crossover between psychology and sociology, culture and nature. But unlike Freud, Mirbeau dispenses with a proper scientific basis (other than a vague post-Darwinian notion of struggle and conflict), preferring to retreat into a satirical distance achieved by the use of a multiplicity of interlocutors, most of whom are highly suspect or plainly ridiculous.

Murder, we learn from this prologue, is a vital instinct akin to 'l'instinct génésique' (44) (Since the term murder is not employed in a legal sense, it seems to be synonymous with aggression or destructiveness.) A philosopher adds that 'le besoin de tuer naît chez l'homme avec le besoin de manger et se confond avec lui' (52); mankind is a predatory species, in other words. However, this philosopher is a Lombrosian physiognomist, ever ready to unloose 'l'avalanche de ses théories' (52); a clear signal that it would be unwise to see his views as more than reductivist outpourings. Thus he needs only to observe people in the street to detect how most 'portent, visibles, les stigmates de cette fatalité physiologique qu'est le meurtre' (46). Ontogeny leads rapidly to sociology and the function of human society. As already noted in the previous chapter, this function seems contradictory. On the one hand, murder is the basis of most imaginable social institutions ('l'industrie, le commerce colonial, la guerre, la chasse, l'antisémitisme', that is all the 'exutoires légaux' invented by civilisation (44–45)). Yet on the other hand, society rigorously forbids individual initiative in this area, condemning 'des assassins qui n'ont fait, en réalité, que se conformer aux lois homicides qu'elle édicte' (53).

This discussion is thus a curious mixture of paradoxical jibes and moralising pessimism. Words like 'stigmates' and 'fatalité' suggest the grafting of a secularised form of original sin on to biological determinism (words such as sin and soul recur throughout the book, in fact). To sum up the argument, we gather that civilisation, the collective grouping of humankind for mutual aid and protection, actually amounts to repression and that the law codifies barbarism (the basic tenet of *Le Jardin des supplices*). Yet the solitary individual is a 'brute homicide' (49), menaced by 'des régressions vers l'époque des antiques barbaries' (50). The vicious circle is inescapable, it would seem. The attraction which Mirbeau felt towards anarchism was doubtless due to the solution it appears to offer to this dilemma. The doctrine is utopian at best, unachievable at worst, but its essentialism is deeply comforting. Like Sade, Mirbeau reveals in *Le Jardin des supplices* a fascination for disorder and the universal transformation of matter, in which the individual consciousness is annihilated, yet unlike the Marquis clings desperately to a sentimental humanism (for instance, the narrator of his novel seeks in vain for redemption through love). Richard D. Sonn has argued that the anarchist vision is based on the myth of a return to a pre-lapsarian human essence, the fall being represented by political authority and economic exploitation: 'Not an economic but a spiritual revolution was tendered' (1989: 267). Significantly, for all his apparent materialism, Mirbeau believes in absolute concepts like Beauty, 'immuable et éternelle comme la Matière dont elle est la forme revivante en nous et synthétisée' (*Correspondance avec Pissarro*, 196), while simultaneously feeling nausea at the grosser organic manifestations of matter. At the very time he was chronicling in excruciating detail the multiple tortures of the garden as a writer of fiction, as a journalist he had joined combat on behalf of Dreyfus and his allies, observing one beneficial effect of the Affair was 'd'avoir donné à beaucoup d'entre nous, trop exclusifs ou trop sectaires, dans leur compréhension de la vie sociale, un sens plus large de l'humanité, un plus noble et plus ardent désir de justice' (*L'Affaire Dreyfus*, 161).

Genet observes in his preface to *Le Balcon* that the writer does not have 'pour fonction de trouver la solution pratique des problèmes du mal. [...] Mais l'œuvre sera une explosion active, un acte à partir duquel le public réagit, comme il veut, comme il peut' (1979: 16). Consequently, to compare the intellectual programme of *Le Jardin des supplices* with scientific or philosophical studies of human aggression by authors such as Konrad Lorenz or Anthony Storr is unlikely to be very fruitful. Mirbeau's primary aim is to set in motion the fictional machinery of his novel, to move from debate to voyage, from voyage to the infernal Eden of the garden. Nevertheless, whatever the text's philosophical shortcomings, we should not forget that the narrator claims of his story that 'C'est de l'histoire contemporaine' (63). Are we then to read the book as a serious reflection on politics (the politics of opportunism and colonialism, in particular)? Politics which the author defined elsewhere, in a wider context, as 'l'art de mener les hommes au bonheur', even if, 'dans la pratique, elle n'est que l'art de les dévorer' (*Les Ecrivains*, II, 26). An attempt to answer this question will conclude our discussion of the novel.

Political corruption fascinated Mirbeau and his contemporaries, just as it continues to appal and fascinate us. Hence the success of the revival in 1995 of *Les Affaires sont les affaires*, which ran for several months to packed houses at the Palais Royal in a lively production by Régis Santon. As ministers continue to rise and fall and move from boardroom to parliamentary chamber to prison cell, Mirbeau's satirical barbs against the Third Republic seem equally applicable to the Fifth. *L'Express* headlined a review of the play by Philippe Alexandre 'On applaudit la corruption' (2 March 1995), correctly stressing the ambiguity of our response to the devious, megalomaniac businessman Isidore Lechat, who in many ways becomes a powerful, heroic figure. The spectacle of political corruption is both derisory and sublime. Writing to Camille Pissarro about the Panama scandal in 1892 (in which most of France's elected representatives appeared to have taken substantial bribes), Mirbeau observed that 'Il y a encore de quoi rire, sur la terre, pour les hommes de bonne volonté'; while the following month he perceived in the business a drama 'plus beau que du Shakespeare' (*Correspondance avec Pissarro*, 125, 132). In *Le Jardin des supplices*, the politician Eugène Mortain (whose dishonesty is axiomatic) is a far more seductive personality than the narrator, whom he dominates in much the same way as Clara does in the second part. Mortain argues precisely that 'L'honnêteté est inerte et stérile, elle ignore la mise en valeur des appétits et des ambitions, les seules énergies par quoi l'on fonde quelque chose de durable' (93).

Readers of *Le Jardin des supplices* may be surprised to discover that Mirbeau's attitude towards colonialism fourteen years previously, in his *Lettres de l'Inde*, was considerably more positive (always assuming that one accepts that the anonymous author of these articles was indeed Mirbeau). This is to some extent explained by his dependence on the patronage of François Deloncle, a proponent of colonial expansion. British imperialism is however seen with hostility in both works, the author of the *Lettres de l'Inde* referring to 'Le caractère britannique, fait de morgue, de dégoût et d'hypocrisie' (77) But in his remarks on ethnography, he is all in favour of the racial purity maintained by the caste system, a perfect practical expression of 'La loi suprême de la lutte pour la vie' (67). Michel and Nivet find such doctrines 'stupéfiant sous la plume de Mirbeau' (108), although his views on race were very much those of his age.

Le Jardin des supplices does in fact contain textual echoes of the *Lettres de l'Inde* (the pattern of the journey to Ceylon aboard the *Saghalien* is set in the earlier work, just as it is in the episodes of 'En mission' published in *L'Echo de Paris* in September 1893). And the later novel does of course express enthusiasm for colonialism: but it is transferred from the narrator to secondary characters, whose perspective the modern reader is hardly likely to share. Everything depends on tone and critical distance. As has been already suggested, Mirbeau's novel shifts from being a social tableau (which is admittedly closer to the ironic manner of Georges Darien in *Le Voleur* (1897) than to Zola's more ponderous naturalism), towards a more Baudelairean allegory (the book in a sense expands in fictional form the symbolic journeys of the poems 'Un voyage à Cythère' and 'Le Voyage'). In this context, unlikely though it may at first seem, we should return to a point briefly alluded to earlier, that the book is a sort of parodic fairy story. The epithet 'féerique', and related words, actually occur with surprising frequency in *Le Jardin des supplices*.

A likely explanation is that the exotic exerts an enchanting allure, while proving on closer inspection to fulfil nightmarish terrors. Mirbeau's rather ponderous satire reduces the 'missions civilisatrices' of colonists to licensed homicide (see for instance the macabre boasts of the explorer in chapter six of 'En mission'). Technology plays a key role. An English artillery officer claims to be the inventor of the dum-dum bullet, named after an Indian village, and possessing the inestimable advantage of penetrating the bodies of a dozen men and reducing the lot to '[des] tas de chair en bouillie et d'os littéralement broyés'; such a device would have been highly useful in France during the repression of the Paris Commune. Taking the notion to its ultimate conclusion, it is suggested that the ideal bullet would totally annihilate its victims (it could be called 'la balle Nib-Nib'). In the meantime, the officer finds the devastating effects of his invention to be 'Magique, vraiment!'. And Clara sees in the weapon 'un nom de fée dans une comédie de Shakespeare... La fée Dum-Dum!... cela m'enchante... Une fée rieuse, légère et toute blonde, qui sautille, danse et bondit parmi les bruyères et les rayons de soleil...' (119–21).

Such an example shows how Mirbeau exploits contemporary allusion in his own peculiar brand of literary satire. The bullets were indeed manufactured in the town of Dum-Dum, near Calcutta, and designed with a soft nose which expanded on impact to cause extensive damage; as a result, their use was banned by the Hague Conference in 1899. However, the British War Office and Admiralty protested against the abandonment of this asset in their struggle against savage nations; as a result, 'the Hague Convention banned the dum-dum from civilized warfare, but left it to be used against wild animals or wild men'. The bullets were extensively used in putting down a rebellion in Zululand in 1906, described by the historian V. G. Kiernan as 'one of the most ghoulish episodes in all the annals of the empires' (1982: 156–57, 119).

Mirbeau's fantasies of destruction were thus outdone by historical reality (his own observation to this effect was noted in the last chapter). The sadistic inventions of *Le Jardin des supplices* were parodied by Reboux and Müller in their well-known series *A la manière de* ... . In their story 'Pour les pauvres' (1913), the narrator visits a factory which turns the bodies of the poor into industrial products: blood becomes iron tablets, teeth piano keys, babies' skins book bindings, fingers hair curlers. But this attempt to match Mirbeau would itself be easily surpassed by the infamous achievements of the Third Reich a generation later. In any case, self-justifying appeals to historical fact may do little to excuse the equivocal complicity found in the literary text. Jean de Palacio has shown recently in *Les Perversions du merveilleux* (1993) how the fin de siècle drew the fairy story into its obsessions with degeneration and progress; Mirbeau's *La 628–E8* inspired Emile Bergerat to write a 'Cendrillon en automobile'. Fairy stories are supposedly written for children, and usually bypass conventional rules and laws. Mirbeau's garden represents the expression of law at its most hideous (and the garden by definition equates to nature contained by culture), yet it also stands for an inexpressible paradise outside or preceding the law. Hence the narrator's frequent invocation of the unsayable and the oneiric. For all his bravura descriptions, 'il est impossible d'en rendre avec des mots la douceur infinie, la poésie inexprimablement édénique'(186). 'Comme sous la baguette d'une fée' there emerges an 'enchantement floral', presided over by Clara, the 'fée des charniers' (186, 201, 228).

Freed from financial, familial or social responsibility, seeking to fulfil her every wish, Clara belongs to no recognisable adult world. Her sadistic joy is explicitly compared to that of a 'baby à qui sa gouvernante vient de permettre de torturer un petit chien' (149). The narrator's sexual relationship with her merits only the most cursory references; far more space is devoted to the erotic spectacle of torture and self-abasement. Clara reduces the narrator to her own infantile perspective: 'Vous êtes un enfant!', she exclaims, calling him 'Pauvre bébé', 'petite chiffe adorée', or even 'petite femme' (134, 148, 155). He in turn wonders whether she is not a child of his own nightmares, a fantasmatic projection (247). The other thus becomes a solipsistic illusion. For all its satirical detail and lurid exoticism, *Le Jardin des supplices* brings us back to Huysman's *A rebours* and the reclusive fantasies of des Esseintes. Like Huysmans' protagonist, however, Mirbeau's narrator is devastated by his experience and forced to return to the banal regimentation of Western society, despite his mockery of its duplicitous conventions, his laughter 'où l'ironie grinça, comme une vieille porte dont les gonds sont rouillés' (58). The novel closes with scenes of hallucinatory orgies, where crazed women violate and are violated by an 'Idole aux Sept Verges'. There is no escape in the Orient from the degenerative cycle of desire and destruction. Whatever its pettifogging meanness, the Third Republic seems infinitely safer and saner than such hypertrophic luxuriousness, as we shall see.

Chapter Four
In My Lady's Chamber

> Bien sûr que c'était une rude salope que Mme la comtesse!
>
> (Octave Mirbeau, *Le Calvaire*)

Readers of Mirbeau's first accredited novel, *Le Calvaire* (1886), will recall that Juliette Roux, the femme fatale who drives Jean Mintié to the final station of his calvary, abandons the running of their opulent apartment on the rue Balzac to three debauched servants: a cook who is 'sale, avide, grincheuse'; a charwoman, la mère Sochard, 'qui prisait sans cesse, se saoulait effroyablement'; and a chambermaid, Célestine, 'effrontée, vicieuse', who entertains her mistress by recounting 'les intimités malpropres des maisons où elle avait passé' (177). Célestine is also the name of the sister of the libertine surgeon Rodin in chapter six of Sade's *La Nouvelle Justine* (1797), 'une mégère, grande, mince, bien faite, brune et très velue, les yeux expressifs, la physionomie la plus lubrique; le clitoris fort long' (cited by Lacombe, 1974: 252); she assists her brother in his atrocious experiments, one of which involves vivisecting his daughter. (Perhaps a more distant relative is *La Celestina*, the satanic panderess of the early sixteenth-century drama attributed to Fernando de Royas.)

The eponymous heroine of Mirbeau's *Le Journal d'une femme de chambre* (1900), the novel with which he greeted the new century, presents herself as 'Un peu grande, peut-être, mais souple, mince et bien faite... de très beaux cheveux blonds, de très beaux yeux bleu foncé, excitants et polissons, une bouche audacieuse' (41). Her journal focuses on sexual licence and social power, both upstairs and downstairs, and thus makes her a direct descendant of her namesakes, even if her eventual surrender to male domination leads to a less horrific dénouement. As Hubert Juin remarks, Célestine, 'cette Juliette-Justine, a quitté les châteaux fermés des libertins de Sade pour les enfers parfumés à la Paul Bourget des boudoirs et des hôtels du Paris 1900' (preface to *Sébastien Roch*, 19). Proper (or improper) names in fact play a key role in Mirbeau's fictionalised analysis of class and servitude; the novel is ostensibly set in the provinces, in a Norman village near Louviers, but much of the plot consists of episodes from Célestine's earlier career in Brittany, Paris and elsewhere. Our discussion will therefore concentrate first on these onomastic aspects, before considering the psychology and physiology of passion presented in the book and the significance of its fragmented structure.

Much like an eighteenth-century novelist, Mirbeau prefaces *Le Journal d'une femme de chambre* by claiming to be only the editor of a manuscript written by Mlle Célestine R.... And he deplores the editorial corrections which have reduced the original force of the text. That Mirbeau is evidently concealed behind this quasi-anonymous person is however indicated by his dedication of the book to the investigative journalist Jules Huret. Here he tells us that we will read a 'livre sans hypocrisie', in which will parade a set of figures 'étrangement humaines', akin to those which feature in the 'longue suite d'études sociales et littéraires' published by Huret himself. Like Huret, the author will contemplate once more 'les masques humains' and convey 'cette tristesse et ce comique d'être un homme' (27). *Le Journal d'une femme de chambre* is at once a reflection on domestic service, social promotion, and the function of writing in late nineteenth-century French society. The reference to Jules Huret doubtless represents the payment of some personal debt, but the name of this once celebrated but now forgotten journalist (remembered principally for his books on naturalist novelists) acquires a symbolic significance through its very anonymity, for the anonymity of this writer is the equivalent of that of Mirbeau's servant author at least for the modern reader. This is their reward for honest, uncompromising work and observation; an ideal of obscurity to be contrasted with the more illustrious name which we have already encountered, Paul Bourget, an author oft cited in the novel, in effect both a real and a fictitious personage who embodies the perfidiousness of the writer who has won worldly and literary success by selling out to the mendacious formulas which sustain the illusions and vanity of the established order. (A novel called *Les Mémoires d'une femme de chambre* was published anonymously by Dentu in 1864, anticipating some of Mirbeau's themes. Jules Vallès reviewed it in *Le Progrès de Lyon* and found it singularly lacking in piquancy. (*Œuvres*,I, 1975: 334, 1345))

Like the maidservant, then, the writer serves the bourgeoisie which buys his work; like the maid, he deals in other people's dirty business. As Mirbeau remarked, the journalist offers himself to a paymaster, although the sacrifice of independence and honesty does not have to be a corollary.

As for the servant, does she have other options than the bestial abnegation of Flaubert's ironically named Félicité in 'Un cœur simple', or the prostitution into which Célestine's sister Louise vanishes? Is honesty a meaningful concept, in any case, in a society where criminality wears the mask of facile virtue? Such are the questions raised by Mirbeau's satirical panorama, through the voice of a character usually condemned to silence and doubly exploited by the laws of caste and sex.

Le Journal d'une femme de chambre contains a multiplicity of names: proper names, names disfigured, historical, fictitious, truncated, or connotative. By making Célestine into an amalgam of Justine and Juliette, Sade's complementary sisters, for instance, Hubert Juin was suggesting that Mirbeau's heroine is torn between vice and virtue, good and ill fortune, becoming in turn victim and agent, exploited object and perceptive subject. Like the protagonist in *Le Jardin des supplices*, Célestine R... has no real surviving family or name (as she reveals in chapter five; hence perhaps the appeal for her of sentimental novels like Hector Malot's *En famille*). In this case, however, she is not merely a disillusioned, declassed individual, but the representative of a whole class or underclass, which is ever ready to seek promotion to the petty bourgeoisie and conquer a new identity by escaping the vast anonymous mass of servants. The social historians Guiral and Thuillier tell us that in 1881, domestic servants represented 3.1% of the population in France; in other words, over a million individuals out of a population of thirty-six million. Moreover, around the end of the century, half the women who became prostitutes were servants gone to the bad; in Paris 2,000 former maids were officially registered each year as prostitutes.

While servants were marginalised socially and legally, for their masters their employment was a means of asserting bourgeois status, however limited one's financial resources:

> Avoir un ou des domestiques assure un certain confort moral: cela donne exactement la mesure de la place dans la hiérarchie sociale et rappelle la toute-puissance de cette hiérarchie; on a quelqu'un à commander et dont le devoir d'état est de vous obéir en tout. (Guiral & Thuillier, 1978: 198)

Anne Martin-Fugier has estimated that around 1900, a lower middle-class household with an income not exceeding 3,000 francs a year might spend

500 francs on the wages of a maid (compared say with 800 francs on rent). Such expenditure may strike the contemporary reader as superfluous, in purely practical terms; yet it granted the master the luxury of enjoying 'l'éternelle, patiente, torturante exploitation d'un pauvre être sans défense' (321), to cite the partial analysis which Célestine herself offers of the moral and economic power relationship involved.

Le Journal d'une femme de chambre, needless to say, is a tendentious work. Nonetheless, Mirbeau seems in most cases to have respected the facts, however bizarre they may at first appear. For example, Martin-Fugier informs us that 'Débaptiser et rebaptiser les domestiques était une habitude chez certains maîtres' (1979: 353). This custom is mentioned several times by Célestine, from the opening chapter of the novel. M. Rabour prefers to call Célestine Marie: 'c'est court... Et puis, toutes mes femmes de chambre, je les ai appelées Marie' (37). In other words, for such an employer, servants belong to an interchangeable series where individual personal identity is unimportant. More precisely, any trace of personal identity is removed from the start of the relationship. In this instance, M. Rabour proves to be more interested in the chambermaid's boots than her person. He insists on polishing them himself, kisses them, kneads them, caresses them, demanding 'd'une voix d'enfant qui pleure' (39) that Célestine hand them over so that he can sleep with them. Four days later, Célestine finds him dead in bed, with one of her boots clenched between his teeth.

The apparent servitude of the servant obliged to comply with her employer's most bewildering whims is thus set against and often overridden by another type of servitude: enslavement to insane passions. Throughout the novel, economic and social oppression is interlinked with the hell of vice, so that winners and losers frequently change places. M. Rabour pays a heavy price for his fetishism: not only does he have to bribe the chambermaid with two louis for her to accept his transaction, but this new contract effectively reverses the habitual master-servant relationship. The master takes on the task of polishing boots, supposedly a humiliating one (hence presumably its importance in establishing military discipline), kneeling down to unlace them, supplicating in a wheedling, childish manner for gratification. If one moves beyond empirical, behavioural observation, one may find that psychoanalytic explanations of fetishism can be as mysterious and unlikely as the practice itself. Emily S. Apter suggests, in respect of this episode (memorably transferred into Buñuel's film of the novel), that 'la bottine opère comme «cache-sexe» de l'invisible phallus féminin qui acquiert, par contiguïté, la valeur d'un substitut de substitut' (1987: 143). Perhaps the key element is indeed metonymic: in the transfer of erotic significance, the container replaces the contained, the boot being substituted for the foot, body or sex of the woman. As a true puritan, Mirbeau considers such displacement of sexual energy as both infantile and dangerous: after regressing to a childlike state of submission before the servant, M. Rabour then expires.

Just as servants play a central role in the bourgeois economy but possess only variable first names, without benefit of a family name, so too sex and related matters are omnipresent but rarely named explicitly in *Le Journal d'une femme de chambre*. We see Célestine dressing as a man in M. Coco's suit and laughing so much at the spectacle that she deposits 'des traces humides' in his trousers (94). We read the description of the mutilated body of the child Claire, whose 'pauvres petites parties', violated by a woodman's axe handle, 'n'étaient qu'une plaie affreusement tuméfiée' (178). Such details suggest that when Mirbeau is prepared to venture into taboo areas, he needs the assistance of humour or violence to justify the transgression. This is apparently the opposite reaction to that of the gossiping hags who discuss the murder of Claire at the grocer's: for these 'créatures', the rape attenuates the killing, 'car le viol, c'est encore de l'amour' (179), a conclusion which Célestine does not seem to accept.

Humour is less equivocal. The comic effect arises from the refusal to name something explicitly (one of Célestine's favourite euphemisms is to say that her masters are, or are not, 'portés sur la chose'). The joke about the venomous, nameless dildo, relevant in this context, has already been mentioned. Not only would the mistress prefer to deny her connection with the incriminating instrument, but she should have declared that it belonged to the maid; Célestine, however, prefers such jewels 'au naturel' (131). In spite of the echoes of Sade which can be detected in novels like *L'Abbé Jules*, *Le Jardin des supplices* and *Le Journal d'une femme de chambre* (outlined by Michel Delon in *Octave Mirbeau*, 1992: 393–401), Mirbeau does not share his predecessor's predilection for obscene anatomical monosyllables. Célestine in fact retains a yearning for purity and innocence as she explores moral turpitude. 'Me voilà propre', she concludes ironically, as she sums up her lugubrious provincial existence in a village where both the inhabitants' souls and the sky are equally 'crasseux' (63).

To return to the naming of individuals rather than parts, we discover, then, that masters or mistresses 'ont tous cette bizarre manie de ne jamais vous appeler par votre nom véritable' (37). The maid can be called 'Mary' or 'Marie' to avoid confusing her in the household with 'des filles, des cousines, des chiennes, des perruches qui portent le même nom' (241). She has no right to keep a name which sounds too bourgeois; thus Jeanne 'n'est pas un nom de domestique... c'est un nom de jeune fille' (305). However, the function of proper names extends beyond such quixotic baptismal rites in Mirbeau's novel.

Certain characters remain entirely anonymous. This is usually because their social category suffices to identify them. They may belong either to the exploiters (like the rapacious old shopkeeper betrayed by the back of her neck), or to the exploited, like the widowed gardener, whose wife died from a miscarriage, induced by the refusal of employers to hire servants with children ('cela dévaste tout... cela fait peur aux chevaux et donne des épidémies' (331)). The sexual exchange can be equally devalued and impersonal: after a hotel employee inspects Célestine 'd'un air de morne désir', she brusquely pushes him into her room and they end the evening 'ivres et vautrés sur le lit' (327). The most fully developed anonymous character is the sacristan, the associate and partial double of the disturbing Joseph. He belongs to the well-established Mirbellian category of 'cloportes ecclésiastiques' (336), a sinister, subhuman species.

Actual historical personages form a rather different type of named characters in the novel. Those whose names carry most symbolic weight are Bourget and Dreyfus. While Bourget defines a specific literary milieu which Mirbeau and his heroine despise, Dreyfus obviously denotes a political context, which forms a historical backcloth to the fictitious action of the book. We should recall that by 1900, Mirbeau had seen Dreyfus convicted again at the Rennes trial in September 1899, despite overwhelming evidence of his innocence and the probable guilt of Esterhazy (himself acquitted early in 1898). Dreyfus was pardoned ten days after the retrial by President Loubet, though his innocence was officially recognised only in 1906. Whatever his earlier anti-Semitism, by the end of the century Mirbeau had placed himself firmly in the *dreyfusard* camp, perceiving in the disgraced Jewish officer a victim not merely of a grotesque miscarriage of justice, but also of a conspiracy hatched by the repressive forces of the army, Church and state.

It is worth rehearsing these facts, well known though they are (or the additional point that 90% of the press was hostile to Dreyfus), if one is to grasp the symbolic role played by Dreyfus as represented in Célestine's *Journal d'une femme de chambre*. This has little to do with the campaign waged on behalf of truth and justice in which Zola and Mirbeau actively participated. Truth in the novel, far from being on the march, has fallen by the wayside. Almost without exception, all the characters display a virulent, irrational hostility towards Dreyfus. The oppressed need a scapegoat on which to unload their hatred and frustration; fanaticism is the only resource of the weak, as Nietzsche observed. Célestine does not share Joseph's anti-Semitism, but as a good patriot has refused service with Labori (the lawyer of Dreyfus and Zola). Joseph believes that Protestants, Freemasons and freethinkers are all 'des juifs déguisés' (137); when Dreyfus returns to France, he exclaims with equally contorted logic: 'Si le traître est coupable, qu'on le rembarque... S'il est innocent, qu'on le fusille' (385).

The novel ends with Dreyfus's return in July 1899. Célestine has escaped domestic servitude by marrying the infamous Joseph (while suspecting him of political agitation, theft and child murder). The latter has fulfilled his social and revanchist aspirations by acquiring a café in Cherbourg patronised by the military. Should we see this conclusion as a new form of bondage for the narrator (she is obliged to dress up as an *Alsacienne* to arouse the customers' patriotic zeal) or as a genuine form of social promotion, however limited her autonomy? Is Joseph's raucous patriotism merely simulated for commercial benefit (hence his observation that 'il n'y a rien comme le patriotisme pour saouler les gens' (386))? Such questions suggest that the book finally offers a moral of a purely cynical variety: patriotism is best measured by its commercial benefits; Dreyfus's innocence is a perfectly good reason to shoot him, for the function of the victim is to be sacrificed.

While on the subject of historical allusions, it should be noted that the book's chronology does not entirely overlap with historical events. Working back from the conclusion set in July 1899, we can situate the opening chapter in September 1898. This calculation is thrown out, however, if other factual references are taken literally. For example, a lecture is mentioned, to be given in October in Louviers by Zola, 'l'immonde Zola' (137); whereas in October 1898, Zola had already been exiled in England for three months. Similarly, Zola's trial is referred to as a future event (174). History is thus compressed for the author's convenience. We need to bear this in mind when interpreting the plethora of historical names found in *Le Journal d'une femme de chambre*. In some cases, admittedly, the satirical allusion and intention are fairly transparent. M. Jules Lemaitre, for all his clericalist sympathies, is a 'petit faune bossu et farceur' (119). Baptising a ferret Kléber or a hedgehog Bourbaki, as Captain Mauger does, can be seen either as a sign of sympathetic anthropomorphism in bestowing glorious names on animals, or more plausibly as debunking the said generals by giving their names to bizarre household pets. Nevertheless, the imbrication of fictitious and real characters can be highly problematic. One could indeed argue that it becomes a central, defining mechanism in the works which follow *Le Journal d'une femme de chambre*, such as *Les 21 Jours d'un neurasthénique* and *La 628–E8*, enigmatic titles of books to which the label novel can be applied only with difficulty. The insertion of a real person doubtless adds what Barthes called a reality effect to the fiction, which gestures towards events of the day (though the sense of the gesture may escape the modern reader). Thus Célestine interrogates Paul Bourget on female psychology and has her waist pinched by Jules Lemaitre. M. Jean, who plays the parts of valet and royalist conspirator, is drawn by Forain and demonstrates alongside Coppée, Lemaitre and Quesnay de Beaurepaire. Perhaps it would be better to talk of an *unreality* effect: by including the adversaries of Dreyfus in his universe of fictional puppets, Mirbeau both ridicules and dehumanises them.

The stratagem is well illustrated by the case of Paul Bourget, that author 'comblé des dons de l'Impuissance', as Léon Bloy caustically remarked (cited by Grojnowski & Sarrazin, 1990: 375). In 1883, Mirbeau described Bourget in *Les Grimaces* as 'ce poète exquis et ce critique rêveur et raffiné' (1927: 42), apparently without irony. Subsequently, their mutual admiration evaporated, as Mirbeau's libertarian tendencies and Bourget's complacent authoritarianism became more overt. The portrait painted by Célestine in her journal in fact rapidly encompasses the degeneration of admiration into scornful disillusion. At first, after listening to the 'ordures vomies' by the women at the grocer's, Célestine congratulates herself that 'la lecture des romans de Paul Bourget' (84) has saved her from such turpitude. The illustrious master has informed her in any case that 'ces âmes-là [...] ne sont pas du ressort de ma psychologie' (118). Yet on rereading Bourget's books, she judges them to be 'faux et en toc' (144) and considers that she herself has a much better acquaintance with the wealthy and luxurious living which so bedazzles the author of *Cruelle énigme*. Like adultery, Bourget has gone out of fashion (205); his writing resembles a basin 'où nagent, parmi du poil et de la mousse de savon... les olives du Calvaire' (266). In the penultimate chapter of the novel, Célestine makes Bourget the emblem of literary vanity and worldly artifice: while the superior servant M. Jean, a 'moraliste de l'office, [...] vidait les pots de chambre... M. Paul Bourget vidait les âmes' (368).

Célestine thus rejects this past master, who is reduced to a mere flunkey pandering to the establishment. This of course parodies the plot of Bourget's best-known novel, *Le Disciple* (1889), where a young intellectual, corrupted by the spurious prestige of a famous philosopher, belatedly realises his error but is overcome by catastrophe. In his preface to the book, Bourget solemnly declared himself possessed by the 'noble espoir de refaire la France' and the urge to praise 'la brave classe moyenne, la solide et vaillante Bourgeoisie' (3, 4). By inventing the character Célestine, Mirbeau has in effect created an anti-Bourget: a female writer, a woman of the people, who rejects the sanctimonious hypocrisy of class superiority, who lives through the senses and the body, and who prefers grotesque comedy to the ethereal refinements of psychological analysis. Before turning to Mirbeau's version of the physiology of love (to use Bourget's terminology), some concluding remarks on the names of characters in *Le Journal d'une femme de chambre*.

As regards the purely fictitious characters, Mirbeau sometimes adopts a nomenclature of a neutral sort (as with most of the servants who appear: Célestine, Joseph, Rose, Marianne, M. Jean, Justin, William, and so on), while in other cases the name chosen invites more immediate deconstruction, usually suggesting an allegorical or satirical reading. Célestine is deflowered at the age of twelve by a certain Cléophas Biscouille, who rewards her with an orange; a decrepit old man selling dog-roses is called le père Pantois; the Lanlaires' bad-tempered neighbour possesses a prodigious, omnivorous appetite and is called Captain Mauger (into which one can read words like 'maugréer', 'manger', and 'ogre'). Such reductive symbolic interpretation can apply to many of the masters. In other words, if the employer attempts to transform the servant into an automaton devoid of will, Célestine reverses the process by presenting her masters and mistresses as a set uniformly characterised by repugnant bodies, ridiculous tics, abject urges and ludicrous names. Employers are often referred to simply by a 'Monsieur' or 'Madame', a purely false mark of respect, particularly when the full name is an absurd one. Hence, as we have seen, the 'nom ridicule et comique' (57) attached to the proprietors of le Prieuré: Lanlaire, permitting a feeble pun which is complemented by their first names Isidore and Euphrasie. Chapter ten of the novel describes a soirée held by the parvenu writer Victor Charrigaud, author of *Leurs jarretelles* and *Les Bigoudis sentimentaux*. These titles set the tone for the parodic parade that follows. Two academicians, Joseph Dupont de la Brie and Isidore Durand de la Marne, are preceded by Sir Harry Kimberly, 'musicien symboliste, fervent pédéraste' (206), who recounts an episode involving wife-swapping between his compatriots John-Giotto Farfadetti and Frédéric-Ossian Pinggleton. French commentators are always determined to identify this burlesque trio as Oscar Wilde, D.G. Rossetti and Burne-Jones (or alternatively, William Morris, if the bartered bride Botticellina is identified as Jane Morris), although Rossetti, Burne-Jones and Morris were all dead when the novel appeared in 1900. As for Kimberly, his affected quips hardly match Wilde's legendary epigrammatic verve; Wilde died in November 1900, a few months after the book appeared. Mirbeau's satire is more effectively demonstrated in this chapter in the character of the anxious arriviste, Mme Charrigaud, whose ritualised social pretensions merit comparison with Proust's Mme Verdurin.

* * *

To sum up the presentation of social class in *Le Journal d'une femme de chambre*, we soon become aware that writing for Célestine is a form of vengeance. The chambermaid becomes a spy or ethnologist within the teratological bourgeois household, one who 'surprend ses maîtres dans toute la saleté, dans toute la bassesse de leur nature intime' (51). Nonetheless, as a social class, servants are entirely devoid of revolutionary potential. They can mock, ape or envy; Célestine notes that 'C'est un fait reconnu que notre esprit se modèle sur celui de nos maîtres' (118). The servant is 'quelque chose d'intermédiaire entre un chien et un perroquet'

(145), 'un monstrueux hybride humain', belonging neither to the people nor to the bourgeoisie (176). He or she acquires 'les criminels appétits' of the bourgeois, 'sans l'excuse de la richesse', and 'garde l'amère grimace de la révolte' (177). Despite the opportunities available, servants rarely take retaliatory action, for they have 'la servitude dans l'âme' (272). For women, only prostitution or social promotion offer alternative options. Célestine justifies her rejection of high-class prostitution not so much through virtue as perversity and lack of willpower. In addition, the chambermaid enjoys some of the prestige of the mistress whom she seeks to emulate. Célestine's real aspirations are indicated by her 'toilette de dame' (76) and opinion that M. Lanlaire lacks dignity when chatting 'familièrement avec des gens trop au-dessous de lui' (98). In the employment agent Mme Paulhat-Durand (whose real name is Joséphine Carp), she easily smells out a former chambermaid and 'la crasse des origines inférieures' (298). Similarly, she is ashamed of the plebeian manners of another mistress, a person 'mal nettoyé par un trop récent luxe' which fails to conceal 'les persistantes boues familiales' (350).

When the situation is reversed, and she becomes the *patronne* of the café, Célestine is equally disgusted by the insolent demands and shameless behaviour of her own maids, who are rapidly dismissed from her service. She aspires to escape defilement and obtain power for herself, rather than to achieve social justice for her peers, in other words. In this context, Mirbeau's own marriage to a woman suspected of having been an upmarket cocotte should be remembered. If biographers are to be believed, his sterile union with Alice Regnault was not dissimilar to the Lanlaires' (including the neighbour who enjoyed hurling stones into his garden). His correspondence with Pissarro reveals that Mme Mirbeau had no scruples about firing her chambermaids, or blaming them for her own social blunders. (Pissarro never forgave Mirbeau when the capricious Alice refused to admit the artist and his son when they turned up unexpectedly at the Clos Saint-Blaise one day in July 1893.)

Célestine's petty bourgeois ambitions may simply entrap her anew. Her phthisical lover M. Georges considers her to be 'une pauvre petite esclave' (153). She may not surrender to her masters, but she surrenders to Joseph. The logic of the novel's conclusion may cause offence: in Renoir's and Buñuel's film adaptations of *Le Journal d'une femme de chambre*, for instance, the final link between Joseph and Célestine is broken, for

Hollywood or surrealist morality apparently did not permit the heroine to marry a thief, rapist or murderer, still less a protofascist. The fact remains that Mirbeau's conclusion delivers a moral, even if it is a disobliging, Sadeian one of happiness attained through crime. Joseph's employers assume, after his fifteen years of devoted service at le Prieuré, that he embodies 'le type du serviteur de l'ancien temps, le domestique d'avant la Révolution' (186). They are mistaken. His loyalty is feigned, to remove the suspicion with which most servants are regarded (as Célestine remarks, every object cries out at them 'au voleur!' (271)), and to allow him time to plan his final escapade — the theft of the Lanlaires' supposedly impregnable silver.

Apart from its financial benefits, this crime offers the additional advantage of violating the masters' intimate being, almost a sort of infanticide (the avaricious Mme Lanlaire gazes at her empty boxes 'comme on regarde son enfant mort' (371)). In becoming Joseph's accomplice, Célestine achieves a more fundamental revenge than that offered by writing. The theft offers an occasion for reflections on economic justice. 'Quel est l'argent qui n'est pas volé?' (382), she asks, in the fashion of the protagonist of Georges Darien's *Le Voleur*. Burglary re-establishes a more equitable order (373); moreover, the Lanlaires had built their fortune on exploitation and swindling (M. Lanlaire's father died in prison, a fraudulent bankrupt). The presumed perpetrator of the crime, Joseph, possesses some revolutionary characteristics — those of the extreme right (xenophobia, militarism, sadism, ruthlessness). When he talks of revolution favouring cafés (226), he does not mean the regenerating dawn of anarchism. But his ideology is pretty rudimentary, if not purely opportunistic; it his implacable sadism that is more disturbing, all the more so because of its obvious appeal to Célestine. However, it is worth noting that there is no formal proof in the text of Joseph's guilt of any crime. Célestine indeed marries him because she presumes he is guilty and even fears at times that she may be mistaken and have committed herself to a harmless fanatic (382).

Passion is always excessive and disruptive in Mirbeau's works. Hence her eroticisation of crime, in the statement that 'un beau crime m'empoigne comme un beau mâle', in 'un viol douloureux et pâmé de mon sexe' (372). The economy of the text and Célestine's perverse imagination evidently incline us to believe that Joseph is a genuine monster, despite his taciturn refusal to admit anything. For the besotted chambermaid, he is part werewolf, part devil (185, 188), yet enjoys a complete 'tranquillité morale' (383). There are besides other suspects in the case of the murdered child: her father, the sacristan, M. Lanlaire. Nothing in Mirbeau's novel justifies the modifications introduced by Buñuel and his scriptwriter Jean-Claude Carrière, when they show us Joseph mishandling the murder victim Claire in the kitchen, to establish a linking motivation absent from the book, and subsequently cast Célestine in the unexpected role of detective and informant, when she visits the scene of the crime and drops a metal stud from Joseph's boot in a fruitless attempt to incriminate him.

What can be asserted more certainly about the moral perspective of *Le Journal d'une femme de chambre* is that 'si infâmes que soient les canailles, ils ne le sont jamais autant que les honnêtes gens'; and from the woman's viewpoint, all men are rogues (367). Attraction or conflict between the sexes take a very physical or physiological form in Mirbeau's fiction, as they frequently do in post-naturalist fiction. Disappointment and frustration find expression in specific behavioural or bodily (mal)functions, just as the leprous tenements and slimy staircases which supply the social decor seem themselves to be infected with some pervasive psoriasis (witness the description of an appropriately symbolic 'taudis malsain' in chapter fifteen (297)). Previous critics have analysed in some detail how Mirbeau presents decay and desire in this novel. The editor of the Garnier-Flammarion edition, Michel Mercier, argues that two series of metaphors are used in *Le Journal d'une femme de chambre* to express the heroine's experience of moral and physical defilement: one relates to 'le pourri', rottenness, and the other to 'le fauve', the musky, potent appeal of the predator (23–24). Such notions are explored in further, persuasive detail by Serge Duret in 'Eros et Thanatos dans *Le Journal d'une femme de chambre*' (*Octave Mirbeau*, 1992: 249–67). He demonstrates that Mirbeau presents desire as essentially morbid and sterile, exploiting metaphors of dissolution and liquefaction, or alternatively, desiccation and mummification, to give artistic form to this pessimistic vision.

To conclude this discussion, I would like to offer some further illustrations and variants on such themes. As has already been suggested, the collapse of the body relates to the sapping of individual will in a society which places most value on destructive opportunism; at the same time, Mirbeau's exploitation of caricature and the grotesque forms part of his decomposition of the novel as a coherent fictional structure. Female bodies are most vulnerable to disintegration: Rose, Captain Mauger's servant-mistress, is an 'outre ambulante' with her 'sourire épais, visqueux, sur des lèvres de vieille licheuse' (77); Mme Gouin's bosom 'remue comme un liquide dans une bouteille' (82); when one of Célestine's mistresses strips off and reveals her body, 'débarrassé de ses blindages et de ses soutiens, on eût dit qu'il allait se répandre sur le tapis en liquide visqueux' (65). The male seems less prone to such liquefaction. His malfunctioning desire is, however, suggested in an analogous albeit less blatant fashion, notably in the repeated motif of drooling and salivation. A whimsical reviewer summed up the theme of Boris Vian's pornographic thriller, *J'irai cracher sur vos tombes*, as 'Je crache, donc j'essuie'. The same might be said with regard to many characters in *Le Journal d'une femme de chambre*.

The fetishist M. Rabour's mouth is 'tout entière barbouillée d'une sorte de bave savonneuse' (40) as he kneads Célestine's boots. M. Lanlaire also compliments her on her skill at polishing boots, his actual intentions being signalled by gasping and slobbering 'comme s'il eût mangé une poire trop grosse et trop juteuse' (123). His wife, who refuses sexual congress with her spouse, has 'des lèvres trop minces, sèches, et comme recouvertes d'une pellicule blanchâtre' (43); M. Lanlaire makes do with the cook Marianne whose 'lèvres pendent et luisent comme la margelle usée d'un vieux puits' (290), a particularly gross image of more accommodating sexuality. When Célestine spurns the advances of another libidinous employer, inevitably we learn that 'une bave menue moussait à ses lèvres' (260). Frustrated or perverted desire seems to inflict an infantile regression on its victims. A fourth case, that of the phthisical adolescent M Georges, further illustrates such defective orality. At first sight, his relationship with Célestine is more positive. He inspires the writing of her journal, and she forestalls the onslaught of his malady, 'comme une nourrice à qui l'on a confié un baby presque mort' (151). But sexual intimacy destroys the fragile equilibrium of the couple, where Georges's social superiority is offset by Célestine's maternal role: nourishment degenerates into a curious vampirism, as she becomes an incestuous ghoul draining off Georges's vital substance, finally gulping down 'un gros, immonde crachat sanguinolent' (160) which he coughs up in his dying moments. Reduced to skeletal emaciation, he expires and spews a final gush of blood in her face

(164). Saliva, then, in this perilous exchange of bodily fluids, is not a euphemistic substitute for sperm, which renews the life cycle, but an anticipatory leakage of life-sustaining nutrients. Interestingly, neither Joseph nor Célestine suffer from the loss of substance which affects other characters. The predatory Joseph, with 'sa bouche large... son énorme mâchoire de bête cruelle et sensuelle' (181), bleeds his victims (whether the ducks or the child Claire), without remorse; and he knows how to 'arranger une femme' (200), as he puts it. For all her sado-masochistic transitions 'de l'état de bête d'amour à l'état de bête de servage' (254), Célestine retains her corporeal autonomy. Her trajectory is the obvious unifying factor in the journal, which otherwise tends to degenerate into an endless display of macabre experiences and grotesque automata, as she observes in the penultimate chapter (367). The 'histoires en gigogne' (Noël Arnaud, 'Folio' edition, 1984: 25) which make up *Le Journal d'une femme de chambre* reflect the fragmentary nature of Célestine's nomadic experience, but also of course Mirbeau's own practice as a journalist recycling material in the less ephemeral genre of fiction. Her primal experiences, which perhaps explain the macabre repetitive quality of subsequent episodes, are the death of her father, a Breton fisherman drowned at sea, whose corpse she saw crowned with seaweed (115), and her sexual initiation on a bed of seaweed by his replacement, Cléophas Biscouille, whom she recalls with 'une grande tendresse' (117) despite his brutality.

Célestine revisits such episodes and yearns to retrieve lost innocence; as she says, she needs only a little affection for her to feel 'revivre en moi une âme d'enfant' (145). The novel however offers a dispiriting image of childhood. Normal reproduction virtually disappears from the account: if the Lanlaires are childless, servants are forbidden to breed, as the numerous references to abortion and miscarriages indicate. Children are perceived as a sort of pestilential vermin. Hence Rose's remark to Célestine that for 'une jolie fille comme vous, [...] un enfant, ce serait un meurtre' (183) and the success of the abortionist Mme Gouin in ridding the area of the *'chiées* d'enfants' (183) which formally polluted it. In effect, adults replace children by regressing to a factitious infantilism. The masters drool like incontinent infants; the mistresses address their maids as 'ma fille'; the latter retaliate by calling their employers 'petit père' and 'petite mère'. M. Xavier calls Célestine 'mon petit bébé' (252), but making love to her whispers 'Petite putain, tu sens maman' (253); Rose admires Captain Mauger's childishly malicious pranks. Unlike the heroine of Buñuel's film, Mirbeau's Célestine rejects Mauger's duplicitous advances, for it is Joseph, with his 'ton paternel' (227), who closes the interminable cycle of inadequate males by returning her to her origins. 'Née de la mer, je suis revenue à la mer' (369). The origins of the novel itself form a curiously protracted cycle, stretching over nine years. Fifteen out of seventeen chapters were first serialised in *L'Echo de Paris* from 20 October 1891 to 26 April 1892, and then reappeared in *La Revue blanche* from January to June 1900 (while the missing chapters two and ten had appeared in *Le Journal* in June 1895, January 1897 and January 1900). The book was finally published by Fasquelle in July 1900 (see Nivet, 1987: 340–41). It has always been a success (150,000 copies were sold in the author's lifetime, 250,000 by the time Buñuel's film came out in 1964), perhaps because Célestine (appealingly reincarnated by Paulette Godard and Jeanne Moreau in the better-known screen versions, although these adaptations were preceded by a silent version and a stage play) is Mirbeau's most fully realised fictional creation.

Nevertheless, *Le Journal d'une femme de chambre* inaugurates a series of works which abandon conventional linear narration and realistic characterisation. Critics like Reginald Carr and Serge Duret have recently provided detailed analyses of the book's structure (see respectively, *Colloque Octave Mirbeau*, 1994: 69–80 and *Cahiers Octave Mirbeau*, 1995: 101–24). Rather than replicate their observations, I refer the interested reader to these articles, which show that twelve of the seventeen chapters contain intercalated episodes from the heroine's past existence, so that 55% of the text actually consists of flashbacks or interruptions. I prefer to turn now to Mirbeau's subsequent writings, which are less well explored yet offer equal illustration of his innovative powers.

Chapter Five
Mirbeau's Hedgehog

> Unflatteringly, it is the primitive insectivores, represented by the hedgehogs, which are the ancestors of the modern primates (which includes monkeys, apes and man).
>
> (Stephen Walker, *Animal Thought*)

Small mammals and their links with humankind fascinated Octave Mirbeau, as the following long extract shows:

Un jour que j'étais descendu à la cave, —Dieu sait pourquoi, par exemple? — je trouvai, au fond d'une vieille boîte d'épicerie, sous une couche épaisse de petit foin, dit d'emballage, je trouvai ... quoi? ... un hérisson. Roulé en boule, il dormait de ce profond, de cet effrayant sommeil hivernal, dont les savants ne nous ont point encore expliqué la morphologie — est-ce ainsi qu'il faut dire? La présence, dans une boîte d'épicerie, de cet animal, ne m'étonna pas autrement. Le hérisson est un quadrupède calculateur et fort «debrouillard». Au lieu de chercher, pour l'hiver, un peu confortable abri sous un dangereux et aléatoire tas de feuilles ou dans le trou d'un vieil arbre mort, celui-ci avait jugé qu'il serait plus au chaud et plus tranquille dans une cave. Notez, en outre, que, par un raffinement de confortable, il avait choisi, pour l'hivernage, cette boîte d'épicerie, parce qu'elle était placée contre le mur, à un endroit précis où passe le tuyau du calorifère. Je reconnus bien là un des *trucs* familiers aux hérissons, qui ne sont pas assez stupides pour se laisser mourir de froid, comme de vulgaires purotins.

L'animal, réveillé par moi progressivement au moyen de passes savantes, ne parut pas non plus s'étonner outre mesure de la présence, dans la cave, d'un homme qui l'examinait indiscrètement, penché sur sa boîte. Il se déroula lentement, s'allongea peu à peu, avec des mouvements prudents, se dressa sur ses pattes basses, et s'étira comme fait un chat, en grattant le sol de ses ongles. Chose extraordinaire: quand je le soulevai et le pris dans ma main, non seulement il ne se roula pas en boule, mais il ne darda pas un seul de ses piquants et ne fronça point les plis barbelés de son petit crâne. Au contraire, à la façon dont il groïnait et faisait claquer sa mâchoire, à la façon aussi dont son nez farfouilleur frémissait, je vis qu'il exprimait de la joie, de la confiance et ... de l'appétit. Pauvre petit diable! Il était pâle et, pour ainsi dire, étiolé, à la manière des salades qui sont restées longtemps dans un lieu obscur. Ses yeux, très noirs, brillaient de l'étrange éclat qu'ont les yeux des chlorotiques, et ses paupières humides, légèrement suintantes, révélaient à mon œil exercé d'étiologue une anémie avancée.

Je le montai dans la cuisine, et, tout de suite, il nous stupéfia par sa familiarité et ses aises d'être chez soi. Il reniflait comme un affamé vers les fricots qui mijotaient doucement sur le feu, et ses narines humaient, avec d'impératives délices, les odeurs de sauces qui passaient.

Je lui offris d'abord du lait, et il le but avidement. Ensuite, je lui présentai un morceau de viande, sur laquelle, dès qu'il l'eut flairé, il se précipita voracement, comme un tigre sur sa proie. Les deux pattes de devant croisées sur la viande, en signe de possession définitive, il la déchiqueta, de coin, en grognant, et son petit œ il noir s'allumait de lueurs féroces. De menues lanières rouges pendaient à sa mâchoire, et son groin se barbouillait de sauce. En quelques secondes, la viande fut engloutie. Une pomme de terre eut le même sort; une grappe de raisin disparut aussitot qu'offerte. Il avala une tasse de cafe, à grandes gorgées retentissantes ... Après quoi, repu, il se laissa tomber dans son assiette, et s'endormit.

Le lendemain, le hérisson était apprivoisé comme un chien. Dès que j'entrais dans la pièce où je lui avais fait une litière bien chaude, il marquait une joie excessive, venait à moi, et n'était heureux que lorsque je l'avais pris. Alors, caressant, ses piquants si bien couchés sur son dos qu'ils étaient doux ainsi qu'un pelage de chat, il poussait de petits cris sourds qui devinrent, en peu de temps, continus, monotones et endormeurs comme un ronronnement.

Oui, il faut que les naturalistes le sachent, ce hérisson ronronnait.

Comme il m'amusait beaucoup et que je commençais à l'aimer, je l'avais admis à l'honneur de ma table. On lui mettait une assiette à côté de la mienne, et il mangeait de tout, exprimant par de comiques colères son mécontement, quand il voyait emporter un plat dont il n'avait rien goûté. Jamais je n'ai connu une personne aussi facile à nourrir. Viande, légumes, conserves, entremets, fruits, il n'était pas un mets qu'il refusât de manger. Mais il avait une préférence pour le lapin. Il le humait de loin. Ces jours-là, il devenait fou; et on ne pouvait le rassasier. Il eut trois indigestions de lapin dont il faillit mourir, la pauvre bête, et auxquelles je dus opposer des remèdes énergiques et de solides purgations.

Le malheur voulut que, par faiblesse, par perversité, peut-être, je l'accoutumasse aux boissons alcooliques. Quand il y eut goûté, il se refusa, avec un entêtement colérique, à en boire d'autres. Chaque jour, il avalait son verre de fine champagne, comme un homme. Il n'en éprouvait aucune gêne, aucun trouble, aucune ivresse. Buveur solide, il «portait la boisson», comme un vieux capitaine. Il prit aussi l'habitude de l'absinthe, et parut s'en trouver bien. Son pelage avait foncé, ses yeux ne pleuraient plus, toute trace d'anémie avait disparu. Et, quelquefois, je surprenais dans son regard, d'étranges préoccupations, et comme des lueurs de luxure. Certain qu'il rentrerait à son gîte, par les belles nuits chaudes je le lâchais dans le bois, à l'aventure, et le matin, dès l'aube, il était là, près de la porte, attendant qu'on lui ouvrît. Presque tout le jour, il dormait d'un sommeil de plomb, réparant ainsi ses débauches nocturnes.

Un matin, je le trouvai étendu sur sa litière. Il ne se leva pas à mon approche. Je l'appelai. Il ne bougea pas. Je le pris dans ma main; il était froid. Pourtant, il respirait encore ... Oh! son petit œ il, et le regard qu'il me lança, qu'il eut encore la force de me lancer, jamais je ne l'oublierai ... ce regard presque humain, où il y avait de l'étonnement, de la tristesse, et tant de choses mystérieuses et profondes que j'aurais voulu comprendre ... Il respirait encore ... Une sorte de petit râle, pareil au glouglou d'une bouteille qui se vide ... puis deux secousses, un spasme, un cri, encore un spasme ... Il était mort.

Je faillis pleurer ...

Je le considérai bêtement dans ma main. Il ne portait aucune trace de violence sur son corps, flasque, maintenant, comme un chiffon; aucun symptôme apparent de maladie ne se révélait. La veille, il n'était point sorti dans le bois, et, le soir, il avait bu joyeusement son verre de fine champagne. De quoi donc était-il mort? Pourquoi cette soudaineté?

J'envoyai le cadavre à Triceps qui l'autopsia. Et voici le petit mot bref que, trois jours apres, je reçus:

«Cher ami,

«Intoxication alcoolique complète. Est mort de la pneumonie des buveurs. Cas rare chez les hérissons.

«A toi.

«ALEXIS TRICEPS.
«*D.m.p.*»

A reader previously unfamiliar with this author's work is likely to react to his contribution to hedgehog lore with a mixture of amusement, surprise and irritation or bewilderment. Two possible guides to interpretation can be found in other, later texts. A chapter of *La 628–E8* (1907) is called 'La Faune des routes' and tells us about the creatures encountered along the roadside as the narrator journeys through Northern Europe in his motor car. He comments: 'J'ai, pour les animaux, une tendresse de neurasthénique et de misanthrope. Leurs souffrances me font horreur' (274). Nonetheless, the motor car invariably brings death and destruction to most animals that cross its path. And in the first chapter of *Dingo* (1913), when the narrator receives a mysterious parcel that turns out to contain the eponymous antipodean canid, he remarks: 'J'ai l'horreur des mystifications et je manque de l'esprit qu'il faut pour en rire' (15).

In my opinion, it is a mistake to overintellectualise Mirbeau and to present him as a writer of coruscating paradoxes and ironies, when in fact he was essentially a journalist who wrote directly and forcefully, avoiding stylistic obscurities. Nevertheless, he had a quirky and quixotic imagination, and considerable fondness for rapid changes of rhetorical tone and ideological position. His contradictions may make his engagement rather suspect, but they are continually engaging. The narrator of *La 628–E8* professes horror at animals' suffering, and then proceeds to recount with considerable detail and relish the number of dogs he has managed to run over. The horror of mystification expressed in *Dingo* is itself a mystifying denial, since the whole book is written in a *fantaisiste* manner, immediately switching for example to a parody of scientific taxonomies and evolutionary theories that offer reductive explanations for civilised customs. One is at first surprised to learn too that many of the events presented as part social documentary, part autobiography are entirely fabricated. Moreover, Mirbeau may never have owned a dingo at all; nor indeed may he have actually written a sizeable part of the novel himself. Thus we are presented with a whole series of mystifications, of which this is perhaps the ultimate mystification.

One needs to proceed, then, in a spirit of light-hearted caution. The narrator of *La 628–E8* categorises himself as a 'misanthrope', suggesting in other words that his affection for animals is set against a corresponding dislike for the human species. He is also a 'neurasthénique', with all its slightly sinister and mysterious fin-de-siècle connotations of neurotic obsession and physiological morbidity. The hedgehog story, I should add, is taken from chapter three of *Les 21 Jours d'un neurasthénique*, published in 1901 (61–65). Mirbeau's mammals may be observed with tenderness, but they usually come — often literally — to a sticky end. What I want to show about Mirbeau through some examples of his fauna falls into three areas. Once again, we discover that Mirbeau is a great humorist, contributing memorably to a genre that flourished around 1900. Secondly, his fascination with the natural world (he was a keen amateur botanist), with the conflict between men and beasts, or man and the beast, between frustrated idealism and agonised materialism, obviously links him to Zola and naturalism as a literary movement, and in a wider context to post-Darwinian worldviews. Thirdly, his constant shift towards allegorising and the absurd, together with his insouciant treatment of the novel and its architecture, suggest that Mirbeau, despite his obvious limitations in range, looks ahead of some of his better known contemporaries towards a more avant-gardist, expressionist sort of writing that permits him to escape the shackles of nineteenth-century realism and anticipate the innovations of say Kafka or Ionesco.

In the first instance, however, we should return to the hedgehog and give it a closer inspection. After all, any literary author demands to be measured by the concrete effect of his words on the page. The narrator of *Les 21 Jours d'un neurasthénique* has ended up in a town in the Pyrenees where he is supposedly taking a cure. He tells us he is called Georges Vasseur. His friend Dr Triceps, a scientist of some repute, now works in the local lunatic asylum. The hedgehog episode, however, takes place earlier (in 1899) and in another location, two years after Triceps' discovery that 'la pauvreté était une névrose' and that incest is the means to regenerate the race (61). What are we to make of this narrator who discovers the hibernating insectivore as he stands on the threshold of the twentieth century? His preliminary rhetorical questions ('Dieu sait pourquoi?', 'quoi?', 'est-ce ainsi qu'il faut dire?'(61)) are themselves pointers to the arbitrariness of his story, or any fiction, and an invitation to observe the proceedings with detached scepticism.

Even the narrator will fail to weep for his deceased hedgehog. Mirbeau's use of similes, in particular, is the source of sardonic humour: analogies are made with other species that are inappropriately appropriate. In other words, the apparent discrepancy between the hedgehog and what it's compared to usually contains a pointed message about human or animal behaviour. Thus we are told that the hedgehog is 'fort «débrouillard»', well able to look out for himself (until interfered with by man, that is) and find a comfortable niche, unlike the 'vulgaires purotins', the destitute rejects from human society who frequently have walk-on parts in Mirbeau's fiction (62).

The narrator shifts as the fancy takes him between veiled mockery of scientific terminology and procedures and an equally mocking claim to zoological technique and knowledge. He wonders whether 'morphology' is the correct term, although later uses the word 'etiolated' and draws attention to his 'œ il exercé d'étiologue' (62) that can diagnose anaemia at a glance. (He spends most of the book anatomising grotesque specimens of humanity, it should be said.) He is able to awaken the animal 'progressivement, au moyen de passes savantes' (62), a 'tour de passe-passe' that with its accelerated and unspecified dexterity suggests a stage magician. Later he asserts boldly that he has empirical proof that hedgehogs purr, challenging naturalists to disbelieve him by emphasising this discovery in its own brief paragraph. The aroused hedgehog, of course, stretches like a cat. No doubt it is a truism that anyone who writes about animals, at least in a literary medium, is likely to be accused of anthropomorphism. Mirbeau's attribution of human characteristics to his hedgehog is jokingly obvious (it takes to strong drink 'comme un vieux capitaine' (64)), but it may be noted that such qualities fit into a rather wider pattern, which essentially contrasts domesticity with a state of nature. The hedgehog, when partly tamed, is like a cat; later on it has become still more civilised, 'comme un chien' (63) and greets its master with a combination of canine and feline behaviour (recognising him like a dog, turnings its spikes into 'un pelage de chat' that invites caresses (63)).

But the call of the wild can still be heard. It defends its food ferociously, 'comme un tigre sur sa proie' (63), and is set loose in the woods to satisfy its nocturnal lusts. All its appetites are awakened, and it no longer resembles the etiolated lettuce to which it was compared when found in its initial vegetative state. Indeed, like the feckless and unfortunate protagonists of Zola's classic naturalist text *L'Assommoir* (1877), the hedgehog is brought down by physiological excess and lack of moral restraint — by alcoholism, gluttony and sex. For Mirbeau too, these are the evils of a nature irremediably perverted by the hypertrophic demands of civilisation. The hedgehog's prodigious appetite and uncouth table manners may be a source of fun (it takes to potatoes, grapes, rabbit, milk, coffee and finally the demon drink, greedily demanding a taste of every dish, and collapsing in glutted stupefaction over its plate at the end of the meal), but it pays a puritanical price for its indulgences and ends up as an alcoholic wreck ('Cas rare chez les hérissons' (65)).

In this sense, the hedgehog is a prototypical naturalist hero: if it is spared the alcoholic Coupeau's famous death dance in *L'Assommoir*, it finishes more like the actor Ginginet in Huysmans' *Marthe* (1876), whom we also leave as a corpse being sliced up on the dissecting table for another demonstration of 'l'intoxication alcoolique complète' (65). Mirbeau works in a more overtly comic mode, and reverses the habitual image of man reduced to the state of animal (Zola's Gervaise dies like a dog in a kennel-like enclosure). Here, on the contrary, the dubious process of domestication has almost brought the hedgehog to fully human status. A brief note of sentimental lyricism is introduced as the hedgehog's 'regard presque humain' offers a despairing glimpse of life's impenetrable mysteries, but the prevailing burlesque tone is restored when its death rattle is compared, appropriately, to the gurgling noise of an emptying bottle and it expires in rather an orgasmic fashion (a series of violent spasms, after which it becomes 'flasque', 'comme un chiffon', a contrast to its earlier 'virile' drinking habits and nocturnal forays to satisfy 'd'étranges préoccupations' (64, 65)).

Might one not indeed just dismiss this piece, along with the whole of *Les 21 Jours d'un neurasthénique*, as a provocative, burlesque fantasy? Perhaps so, but in that case one would also have to dismiss Mirbeau as a writer worth taking seriously, since the story typifies both his comic manner and underlying moral preoccupations. A more pointed and less dismissive question would be to ask whether the fact that Mirbeau portrays a hedgehog, specifically, is significant (could Flaubert's parrot be replaced by Flaubert's budgerigar?). An initial impression might be that this fictional hero, with its omnivorous appetite, dog-like behaviour, and doubtful sexual habits, bears little resemblance to any real hedgehog one might meet. When the editor of an edition of Lamartine's *Premières méditations* tells us that 'L'Isolement' was inspired by the landscape around Milly and wonders if 'un admirateur de Lamartine pourrait tirer profit d'une excursion sur la montagne du Craz' (1965: 25), we are likely to regard this sort of urge to find documentary correspondences as pedantically irrelevant. Unlike Zola, besides, Mirbeau never professed to be writing 'procès-verbaux' (unmediated reports on reality), and retorted to the journalist Jules Huret's enquiry about the waning popularity of naturalism: 'Le naturalisme? Mais je m'en fiche!' (Huret, 1891: 211). This riposte is again, however, at least in part a mystifying boutade. Like Zola, Mirbeau was throughout his career preoccupied by 'la question sociale', or social questions, and with settling a score with the establishment. His writing for the theatre, seen from the other end of the twentieth century, seems in particular to fall into the easily recognizable category of naturalist thesis-drama (the exploitation of workers and orphans, the corruption of big business in *Les Mauvais Bergers*, *Le Foyer*, and *Les Affaires sont les affaires*, for example). In this sense, documentary authenticity was important to him, as it was in much of his journalistic writing. But Mirbeau actually starts to become most interesting when he moves less predictably from document to fictionalising, from autobiographical reminiscing to fanciful invention (thus *La 628–E8* and *Les 21 Jours* belong to no obvious literary category).

If only to help define these boundaries more clearly, it is useful to check the facts about hedgehogs. Unexpectedly perhaps, the study of a scientific monograph on *Erinaceus europaeus* adds quite considerably to one's understanding of Mirbeau's text. My main source is the English translation of a book by Konrad Herter. Here we learn that the hedgehog is probably the most familiar (wild) mammal in Europe, and appears in countless folk tales, often as a rather tricky character. It has about 16,000 spines, which can be erected or laid flat. When Mirbeau uses the verb 'darder' about the hedgehog, it is unclear whether he is erroneously assuming that the animal can launch its spines like missiles, or simply employing the verb to mean 'dresser', to erect a defensive barrier. Nonetheless, most of his observations about the hedgehog, even those that appear purely fanciful, are actually correct. Hedgehogs are nocturnal, solitary animals, often living under hedges. They can be tamed, trained to respond to sounds, and captive hedgehogs are able to identify the smell of their keeper, or his shoes. Indoor hedgehogs would choose a warm spot for hibernation, such as a radiator or stove. To arouse a hedgehog from hibernation takes several hours. Awakening causes disturbance of metabolic processes and great hunger. Though classified as insectivores, 'Hedgehogs eat practically any living creature that they can catch'. Captive hedgehogs prefer fish 'whether raw, boiled or kippered'; they also eat milk, soaked bread, boiled potatoes, rice, fruit, custard and small amounts of chocolate, many hedgehogs gorging themselves on their favourite food (though others are abstemious). Not only that, but according to Herter, 'Hedgehogs are great drinkers'. Disappointingly, however, he adds 'especially of pure water' (1965: 39–40).

A detail that escaped Mirbeau and that no doubt would have appealed to him is that, for practical reasons, 'The penis of the hedgehog is disproportionately long and it can enter the vagina without any danger of her spines damaging his underparts' (47). A hedgehog giving birth is described as 'purring and squeaking' (48). The belief that hedgehogs can milk cows (by dangling from their udders) is folkloric, as are accounts of them transporting windfallen fruit impaled on their spines.

This brief summary indicates that Mirbeau himself, despite his comic, hyperbolic manner, still obeys the naturalists' rules of empirical observation and literary verisimilitude and avoids folklore or fable, at least in the case of *Les 21 Jours*. In the wider context of his writing, this is less apparent. Even here, it is partly a question of how one defines a fable, of the point at which allegorical interpretation takes over from the concrete reality of an observed situation. Flaubert's parrot (in 'Un cœur simple') is, so to speak, polymorphous — both living and stuffed animal, domestic companion and exotic reminder of a loved one lost in foreign parts, and also final symbol of the Holy Ghost. So too, on a less ambitious scale, is the hedgehog — a comic figure, a domesticated insectivore that is abused by the narrator and Dr Triceps, but also a typical example of the individual who succumbs to the destructive effect of instinct perverted by civilisation (like the hero of the earlier novel *Sebastien Roch*, for instance).

* * *

Kafka's specific debt to Mirbeau's novel *Le Jardin des supplices* has been noted by several commentators (see Burns, 1957 & Binder, 1975). In many ways, it is a lot more interesting to read Mirbeau, or other texts anterior to Kafka, retrospectively in the light of Kafka's own enigmatic fables, where animals suffering from existential anguish often play a leading role. Mirbeau published an allegorical tale called 'La Vache tachetée' in 1898 about a man called 'Jacques Errant' who has spent a year in solitary confinement for no reason. Like Kafka's Josef K. he believes naively in justice and therefore in the probability of his own guilt, thinking that 'suspendu à la terreur d'un procès dont j'ignore la cause, [il] faut que j'aie commis, sans m'en douter, un bien grand crime' (*Contes cruels*, II, 379). Finally he is exposed to the dazzling light of the courtroom (unlike Kafka's petitioner in the section of *The Trial* sometimes called 'Before the Law', who waits in vain to be exposed to this radiance) and is sentenced to 'cinquante années de bagne' for the offence of owning a spotted cow. Mirbeau's specific target in this parable was evidently the Dreyfus Affair (the spotted cow as an arbitrary sign of infamy is equivalent to being a Jewish officer), although the obsessive and fruitless ratiocination of Kafka's submissive characters that is anticipated in this tale makes us think that a more compelling moral is that life is a 'cauchemar, [...] pareille à un conte d'Edgar Poe réalisé'; 'Et la plus grande folie est de chercher une raison aux choses', a message delivered by Mirbeau himself in a story of 1890 whose title consists simply of a question mark (*Contes cruels*, I, 156–57).

To return, for the last time, to hedgehogs, before looking at Mirbeau's treatment of other animals, it is interesting to discover in *Grimm's Fairy Tales* two stories that contain premonitory echoes of both Kafka and Mirbeau. In the fascinating and delightful 'Hans the Hedgehog', Hans starts life with some of the disadvantages of Gregor Samsa in 'The Metamorphosis'. Desperate for an heir, his father rashly says he would be happy to beget a hedgehog. But when Hans is duly born half boy, half hedgehog, he is left to lie 'behind the stove for eight years, and his father was tired of him and thought: "If he would but die!"' (1983: 498), a situation that encapsulates the anti-Oedipal scenario of Kafka's story of the son-insect destroyed by a rejuvenated father. However, Hans has more spunk than the enfeebled protagonists of fin-de-siècle literature and rides off to the forest on a cock, where he plays the bagpipes and becomes a successful swineherd. Finally he marries the second king's daughter and becomes a normal man (the first king's daughter pays for her father's broken promise by being stripped and pierced by his spikes, after which she is 'disgraced for the rest of her life' (501)). It is worth noting, given the reflections on the status of the negro on the evolutionary and socio-political scale in the works of Mirbeau and his contemporaries (we recall that a general in *Les 21 Jours* uses their hides for wallpaper), that Hans passes through a transitional stage as a black in his transformation from hedgehog to man.

The second story, 'The Hare and the Hedgehog', is a reworking of the more familiar fable about the contest between the hare and the tortoise. Here the hedgehog shares the taste of Mirbeau's protagonists, since he bets the hare 'A golden louis-d'or and a bottle of brandy' (761) that he will be the victor. The hedgehog does in fact win the race by judicious cheating (his wife doubles up for him on the finishing line), and the hare drops dead from exhaustion. Mirbeau's comment in a later chapter of *Les 21 Jours* that the hedgehog reveals an 'étonnante roublardise' and a 'merveilleuse ingéniosité [...] dans la lutte pour la vie' (136) points very aptly to the moral of this tale. At this point, the narrator of *Les 21 Jours* is about to reveal another important scientific discovery that he has recently made (previous discoveries included 'l'ambulation chez les végétaux' and 'l'autocriminologie de l'araignée' (136) and aroused furious resentment in the scientific community). This turns out to be a prolonged combat between a hedgehog and a viper, which the hedgehog wins. (In fact, such deadly encounters have been attested by naturalists.)

Readers of Mirbeau will of course recall that the voracious hedgehogs of *Les 21 Jours* have a companion in his previous novel *Le Journal d'une femme de chambre*. Célestine's neighbour, the omnivorous Captain Mauger, is described as having 'une tête de carpe' (105). His method of dealing with an unfamiliar creature is to eat it (flowers, insects, worms and snakes all contribute to his diet). He has a pet ferret called Kléber. When Célestine makes the 'diabolic' suggestion that he eat Kléber, principle forces him to agree and he kills him on the spot ('Tu m'en feras une gibelotte, ce soir!' (109)). A week later, Célestine discovers Mauger taming a hedgehog he calls Bourbaki (like Kléber, a famous general, who died a few years before the book was published). Like its master, this creature is also omnivorous; and like its successor in *Les 21 Jours* it too dies 'd'une congestion pulmonaire, pour avoir bu trop de cognac' (225) (as does Captain Mauger's servant-mistress Rose). Following the practice of Maupassant, Mirbeau was notorious for re-using the same material in different places. Jean-Francois Nivet has shown in tabular form the sources of the forty-six stories that make up *Les 21 Jours* (1987: 346, 353–54). The hedgehog episodes derive from newspaper stories published in *Le Journal* in March and April 1896, entitled 'Un peu de science' and 'Lettre ouverte à Alphonse Allais'. The ferret first appears in 'Puvisse Dechavane' in *L'Echo de Paris*, 23 May 1893 (*Contes cruels*, I, 393f.). The reference to Allais and the fragmentary composition of Mirbeau's later books both merit further comment. But to remain with the subject of his fauna, before opening the discussion on to such wider issues, it is interesting to compare the bestiary of the novel *Le Journal d'une femme de chambre* with Buñuel's film inspired by Mirbeau's text. With their penchant for black humour, narrative disrupted by surreal anecdotes, Roman Catholic priests, unconventional sex, and small animals, Mirbeau and Buñuel may seem to have been made for each other. Certainly, Buñuel's version is far more successful than Renoir's sanitised Hollywood adaptation, where most of the bizarreries and nastiness of the characters are sacrificed to a conventional moral ending (the wicked Joseph gets his just desserts). Some modifications to events in the book in the Buñuel film seem justified or at least insignificant. Thus the character M. Rabour is not only a boot fetishist, but also likes to shoot butterflies. The ducks that Joseph tortures in the book become geese in the film. There is a close up of swarming ants, presumably because this is the director's trademark. In the novel, there is an explicit description of the corpse of the murdered child Claire, whose wandering in the woods is left unmotivated. In the film, she is said to be collecting snails. A shot of three snails crawling over her splayed legs brought objections from the censor, although Marcel Martin claims that this image is 'd'une tendresse, d'une pitié infinies' (*L'Avant-scène cinéma*, 1964: 5–6).

As it happens, Buñuel's fixation on snails and ants is shared by Mirbeau, even if they are neglected in *Le Journal d'une femme de chambre*. Chapter twenty of *Les 21 Jours* contains a macabre story about a cultivator of sea snails, who discovers that his molluscs thrive best when fed on human flesh. Predictably perhaps, in his obsession 'il devint farouche, ainsi qu'une bête' (300) and ends up as a victim of his own snails: man becomes beast, and beast eats man, as nature reverses the normal pattern of culture. The disenchanted hero of *Sébastien Roch* spends his days watching an ants' nest, perceiving in this 'une énorme histoire sociale qu'il serait autrement intéressant d'apprendre que les luttes de la République athénienne' (278). Natural history supersedes man-centred political history (recalling Flaubert's dictum that 'l'histoire d'un pou peut etre plus belle que celle d'Alexandre' (*Correspondance*, 1980: II, 763)). It is at this point that Mirbeau and Buñuel diverge. There can be little doubt that Buñuel betrayed the overriding sense of sadomasochistic complicity that infuses *Le Journal d'une femme de chambre* by effectively purifying the heroine (played by a tight-lipped Jeanne Moreau) and changing her relationship with the other characters. In the film, Célestine actually attempts to incriminate Joseph at the scene of the murder. He escapes justice, however, and establishes the café with another woman of obviously dubious virtue. Now Célestine achieves her own promotion to the ranks of the petite bourgeoisie by marrying Captain Mauger. Although he throws out his servant Rose to replace her with Célestine, he too is made into a more palatable character: his omnivorous eating habits are suppressed, and he becomes a bohemian eccentric who enjoys baiting the stiff-necked neighbours for whom Célestine works. Mauger in the novel is a 'grotesque et sinistre fantoche' (282), and Célestine turns down his proposal in favour of Joseph. In the film, grotesque or evil characteristics are rather schematically transferred to easily identifiable political or class enemies (such as the fascistic Joseph and his friend the sacristan, or sexually perverse members of the bourgeoisie like Rabour and Monteil). As Marcel Martin remarks, 'Tout cela n'a rien à voir avec une psychologie tératologique'; on the contrary, 'c'est une vision sociale' (*L'Avant-scène*, 1964: 6). The slaughter of innocents is observed without sadism, whether they are the child, the butterflies or the geese.

Martin's observations seem intended to vindicate Bunuel from charges of pornographic voyeurism and give him an ideological clean bill of health. Unwittingly, he emphasises the differences between Buñuel and his source. In *Les 21 Jours*, Mirbeau's narrator tells us he delights in the mad, the bad and the monstrous. His writing comes to life when he alights upon a 'dernier spécimen d'humanité tératologique' (81) and is able to entrap it with a caricatural verve that at its best achieves a manic, fantastical inventiveness. Visiting the lunatic asylum where Dr Triceps is employed, the narrator remarks: 'Le regard des fous m'effraie par la possibilité d'une contagion' (66). He meets an inmate who has had his name stolen and thinks he's a character in Balzac; a tailor made off with his thought, which resembled a butterfly. In the outside world, we are shown a marquise followed more predictably by 'tous les échantillons de l'animalité humaine' (117). Mirbeau's bestiary reminds us once again of his overwhelming obsession with the Sadeian immorality of nature, an obsession that throws up (or rather constantly regurgitates) two paradoxes. One is the uneasy dualism that sets nature against culture, staking an imperialistic claim for the uniqueness of the human species while simultaneously accepting scientific theories that place man within a nature governed by evolutionary forces. The other is more particular to Mirbeau: he plays the role of the libertarian anarchist who abhors cruelty and oppression with some conviction, yet his books endlessly recycle tales of horror with joyful gusto, so that he appears as much to celebrate as to condemn man or nature's skill in inventing atrocities.

General Archinard, who appears in a mock interview in chapter nine of *Les 21 Jours,* favours the recycling of negroes' hides as wallpaper, as has already been mentioned. Is this Swiftian satire of colonialist atrocities, or something rather more equivocal? 'Je ne connais qu'un moyen de civiliser les gens, c'est de les tuer', he remarks (115). Civilisation accelerates the normal processes of nature so that the terminus of civilised or natural life, death, is reached with an absurd rapidity. The useless molecules, 'la matière inerte', of the blacks, are reassembled into something more economically or aesthetically useful; the same could be done with white criminals ('Du cuir de criminel, [...] il n'y a pas au-dessus' (116)), but the General rejects the suggestion of dyeing them black to appease public opinion in France.

Is the message of these grisly stories, whether they are about hedgehogs or blacks ('presque des bêtes' (115)), that culture perverts nature's laws, or rather that it takes them to an extreme but logical conclusion? Clara, in *Le Jardin des supplices,* defines monsters as superior beings who exist 'au-dessus des mensonges sociaux, dans la resplendissante et divine immoralité des choses' (225). Are the inhibitions of social morality then no more than ideological lies meant to hide from the individual the reality of what Mirbeau calls throughout his work 'la loi éternelle du Meurtre' (*L'Abbé Jules,* 146)? Society, it would seem, is a monstrous carbuncle on the face of nature, hastening nature's destructive work while simultaneously thwarting the individual's chances of short-term fulfilment. Mirbeau's parables constantly retell the same story and suggest a mixture of moral revulsion and nihilistic delight at this discovery.

This message is displeasing, less perhaps because it suggests an absurdist pessimism than because it often seems tritely reductive and also curiously at odds with Mirbeau's own social campaigning, motivated presumably by a more positive ethic. In the chapter called 'La Faune des routes' in *La 628-E8*, he presents a series of pseudo-fables stemming from observation of various animals and their similarities with mankind. If donkeys are men in their independence and courage, men are all too often merely horses, timorous and servile imbeciles. Travelling through the Netherlands, the narrator and his chauffeur attempt to find the residence of Descartes. Needless to say, the unlettered inhabitants have never heard of the famous philosopher, and direct them to the lunatic asylum, a hotel, the cemetery or a house that displays Spinoza's slippers and lenses. This leads the narrator to recall Descartes's radical separation of men from beasts, and La Fontaine's refusal to accept a purely mechanistic conception of animals. But the narrator wonders:

> Qui fut pour elles plus sévère? Le savant qui leur refusait rigoureusement l'intelligence, même la sensibilité, ou le plus charmant de nos poètes, que leur spectacle émerveilla, mais qui ne leur fit parler que la langue de nos vices et de notre sottise? (290)

Mirbeau's most extended exploration of animal characters is his last completed novel, *Dingo*. This is a much more overtly allegorical piece of work than the rather more anecdotal fragments that have been discussed so far. As a result, his complaint about La Fontaine's anthropomorphism might easily be turned against his own text. This is not necessarily a criticism: animals in fables and fairy stories by definition speak the language of human vices and virtues. The question is rather whether they say interesting things. Marcel Aymé notes that a critic of his charming book, *Les Contes du chat perché*, observed with obtuse sagacity that if animals could talk, they certainly wouldn't talk like the animals in Aymé's stories. Anthropomorphism, besides, is not all that easy to define. When Aymé's heroines Delphine and Marinette reproach the wolf for eating lamb, he retorts that they eat lamb all the time. Carnivores are still carnivores, even if some of them use knives and forks (Aymé, 1975: 7, 172).

Not only do men and animals share certain behavioural traits, but also perhaps certain moral characteristics. Konrad Lorenz notes that 'domestic dogs have been selected by man for properties which in human society are regarded as virtues'. The dog fulfils the Christian command to love one's neighbour as oneself, or at least one's master, rather better than most men, and shows a behavioural awareness of guilt that might be called bad conscience. Lorenz's pet dingo, however, lacked this sort of inhibition. He asserts that the dingo 'is a domestic dog gone feral', although in fact there is no concrete evidence for this (in Fox, 1975: x, viii). The origins of the dingo (how it got to Australia, whether it was a true wild dog or partly domesticated) remain obscure; it can enjoy a limited symbiosis with man, although it cannot be fully tamed.

Mirbeau had two dogs he successively called Dingo. Whether they were really Australian dingoes is unclear and perhaps less important than the fact that the hero of the novel is certainly a wild canid who finds himself living in Western civilisation and a vehicle for his creator's by now habitual reflections on its limitations. If man is an uncertain hybrid, neither ape nor angel, so too is Dingo, who is 'ni chien, ni loup' (20), suspended between domesticity and the wild. In this sense, it may seem that to accuse Mirbeau of anthropomorphism (the attribution of human qualities to superior or inferior beings) is doubly inappropriate, if we are meant to accept a truly evolutionary conception of both man and beast: human nature is not radically separate from other species; all are subject to the same materialist determinisms. In fact, Mirbeau introduces evolutionary theories from the beginning of the novel, but the intention is obviously to parody the pretensions and arbitrariness of scientific taxonomies: 'Rien n'est immuable. Tel qui était poisson jadis est devenu oiseau; tel qui fut singe est aujourd'hui pape, roi, ministre, général ou philosophe' (19). Similarly, the causal chain is stretched to absurdly reductive lengths: 'Herbert Spencer, en juillet 1873, découvrit dans la danse du scalp des Fijiens l'origine de la musique, du drame, et même de la biographie' (23).

At the same time, however, Dingo is the free spirit untrammelled by the discontents and inhibitions of civilisation. He is a natural enemy of the brutish peasantry and their domesticated livestock, but also of lawyers and soldiers, since he is endowed with an anarchist's disdain for property and the established hierarchy. Nonetheless, he is undyingly loyal to the narrator, although he himself appears as a member of the ruling, possessing classes with a sentimental attachment to the underdog. Mirbeau's contemporary Jack London has been accused of anthropomorphising animals to an absurd extent in the famous dog stories like *The Call of the Wild* that were published in the decade before *Dingo* (1913). If London is saved by the 'presentational immediacy' of his fiction, which makes him 'an artist of violent action' (James Dickey in London, 1981: 15-16), Mirbeau falters partly because he is unable to give Dingo a convincing canine personality, even an anthropomorphised one. As he says in chapter eleven, 'Dingo n'était ni un chien ni un homme' (217-18). Instead he tends to become a pretext that justifies a succession of anecdotal or allegorical episodes mainly based on his escapades.

The fragmentary composition of Mirbeau's later books has always struck his critics. His biographers Michel and Nivet (1990: 886) point out that he was physically unable to complete *Dingo* and passed the task on to Léon Werth, who wrote the last three chapters (including the eleventh chapter set in Paris, just quoted, which is one of the most lively). Whether Léon Werth had a free hand in this exercise or not remains unclear. In his declining years, Mirbeau was surrounded by a quarrelsome entourage which engaged in mutual recriminations about the master's wishes. The novel *Un gentilhomme* was never finished and the jingoistic 'Testament politique' published on his death in 1917 is often said to be a forgery concocted by his wife and her associates.

A conventional (and perhaps justifiable) response to the hybrid works which Mirbeau published in the early years of the twentieth century is simply to reject them as of little lasting interest. Thus Reg Carr finds what he calls the three novels *Le Journal d'une femme de chambre*, *Les 21 Jours* and *La 628-E8* to be 'inferior in literary quality to most of his previous work' (1977: 134). Personally, I find them superior to the more conventional early novels, precisely because of their diversity, perversity and unconventional blending of fact and fiction. Julian Barnes's well-received novel *Flaubert's Parrot* (1984) cleverly blends fictional biography, literary scholarship and academic spoof around that central, proliferating psittacine figure. (Curiously, the hero of Barnes's first novel, *Metroland* (1981) is a student of French called Christopher Lloyd.) The fictional hero Braithwaite is used to deflate critical pomposities and to settle the hash of a real-life *monstre sacré* like Enid Starkie. We saw that Mirbeau does the same thing to Paul Bourget in *Le Journal d'une femme de chambre*. Mirbeau's humour is no respecter of persons, animals or literary conventions. It is often offensive and distasteful, but also provocative and inventive, the glue that holds together the loose-fitting framework of his disrupted narratives. In his *Anthologie de l'humour 1900*, Jean-Claude Carrière observes: 'De 1880 à 1910, la France a connu la plus grande épidémie de rire de son histoire' (1988: 7). Mirbeau clearly helped spread this epidemic, although curiously his work does not feature in this book (even though Carrière wrote the script for *Le Journal d'une femme de chambre*). A concluding example of Mirbeau's black humour might be his one-act play, appropriately entitled *L'Epidémie* and performed at the Théâtre Antoine in 1898. The ubiquitous Dr Triceps, who diagnoses neurosis as the universal cause of all ills in *Les 21 Jours*, also appears in this rather grating comedy, the plot of which is loosely derived from Ibsen's *An Enemy of the People*, since it is about a town council's deliberations on how to contain a typhoid epidemic that threatens its prosperity. The satire is predictable: the representatives of the people remain unperturbed while the victims are only soldiers in the local barracks. But the death of a bourgeois, a superior species, 'vénérable, gras, rose, heureux', is more disturbing. 'Son ventre faisait envie aux pauvres' (*Théâtre*, I, 275); death should respect the social hierarchy. More interesting than the grotesquely egotistical characters are the occasional absurdities and automatisms of gesture and language that push the play in the direction of Ionesco.

But Mirbeau remains a naturalist, here as elsewhere. Zola offered a definition of naturalism as 'le retour à la nature, l'esprit scientifique porté dans toutes nos connaissances' (cited in Baguley, 1990: 12). Mirbeau's scepticism about the limitations of the scientific spirit is exemplified by a character like Triceps, whose deterministic fatalism is simply a hypocritical guise for leaving the iniquities of the social order undisturbed. In *Dingo* a triple-chinned, porcine vet appears who asserts that rabies is a disease invented by the Pasteur Institute to keep it in business (chapter eleven). Science or its practitioners can cast darkness as well as light, perpetuate rather than dispel mystification. Mirbeau shares the disillusioned pessimism of those late nineteenth-century writers who found man's reinsertion in nature to be a mixture of comedy and catastrophe. David Baguley defines naturalism in a telling phrase as 'the genre of the human genre, a body of literature that views man generically, as a (threatened) species' (1990: 128). He quotes the Goncourt brothers' caustic scatological definition of human reproduction: 'L'homme pisse l'enfant et la femme le chie' (*Journal*, 4 February 1861, cited 1990: 215). In Mirbeau's novel *Sébastien Roch*, the eternal monotony and degrading inevitability of the biological cycle are conveyed in a less excremental but equally typical phrase: 'c'était l'époque où les couples amoureux et enlacés promenaient leurs ruts dans les champs' (340). Elsewhere, we find similar images typical of the lugubrious zoological vision of naturalist authors: a hideous prostitute compared to a toad, a weak-willed protagonist to a 'silencieux insecte', France itself to an 'immense faisanderie', which is despoiled by greedy predators (*Les 21 Jours* (266); *Dans le ciel* (chapter eight); *Les Grimaces*).

Fortunately, Mirbeau's vision of the natural world is not limited to such dispiriting and familiar metaphors. In the story which he wrote about his passion for flowers called 'Le Concombre fugitif', he remarks: 'Les fleurs me sont des amies «silencieuses et violentes» et fidèles. [...] Mais je n'aime pas les fleurs bêtes' (*La Vache tachetée*, 145). The peripatetic cucumber, a sort of vegetable Albertine, is obviously better equipped for survival than the alcoholic hedgehog; so too is a literary manner that sees the advantages of disrupting the earthbound subject matter and conventions of naturalist writing. In a famous essay on Tolstoy's conception of history, Isaiah Berlin quotes an ancient Greek proverb that says: 'The fox knows many things, but the hedgehog knows one big thing' (1953: 9). Whatever the value of his distinction between supposedly centripetal and centrifugal writers, we might well accept that Mirbeau did not know many tricks. For all that he was married to Alice Regnault, the widow of M. Renard and reputedly a foxy lady, Mirbeau was no doubt a hedgehog. In some versions of the fabled race, the contest is between fox and hedgehog, for they are the two most cunning animals. Once again, it is the hedgehog who wins. Mirbeau may well have been a prickly customer, with a fairly short-sighted vision and range; but his barbs retain their sharpness and help guarantee his survival.

Chapter Six
Travelling Man

> Nous dîmes adieu à toute une époque
> (Apollinaire, 'La Petite Auto')

My final chapter focuses on Mirbeau's last completed book, *La 628–E8*, published in 1907, a title as unpronounceable as it is enigmatic. Mirbeau's fondness for numerical titles combining provocation and mystification is also illustrated by the work published six years before *La 628–E8*, *Les 21 Jours d'un neurasthénique*. While *La 628–E8* was in fact the registration number of the author's automobile, one of the principal subjects of the later book, the title of *Les 21 Jours* nominally refers to the period spent by the narrator recuperating in a spa town in the Pyrenees. Whereas *La 628–E8* ranges widely over the highways of time, space and literary genres, *Les 21 Jours* deals with themes of entrapment and impotence. The narrator's stay is seemingly prolonged over far more than three weeks, for he is unable to escape the resort: 'Vingt fois j'ai voulu partir, et je n'ai pas pu [...] je suis envahi, conquis par la neurasthénie' (*21 Jours*, 192–93). Neurasthenia is universalised as 'la maladie du siècle' (257). At the same time, as has already been remarked, the author's own struggle with literary creation is revealed by *Les 21 Jours*, for the book mostly consists of the recycling of forty-six previously published stories, the 'fond de tiroir d'un journaliste', joined together in a 'formidable entreprise de collage' (Nivet, 1987: 343, 345). For the modern reader, the title *Les 21 Jours* also echoes Sade's *120 Journées de Sodome* (although since this work was published only in 1904, it is unlikely that Mirbeau knew it), as well as Maupassant's story 'Mes 25 jours' (1885), which likewise recounts exotic, erotic adventures in a spa town and alludes to the twenty-eight days' training sessions of military reservists.

Despite its anecdotal, fragmentary character, *Les 21 Jours* clearly remains a work of fiction, a collection of remarkably tall stories, for all that Mirbeau continues his practice of the imaginary interview, whereby a historical figure such as General Archinard is ridiculed by an absurdist embroidering on his publicly stated views. Mirbeau's next substantial work, *La 628–E8*, adopts many of the same techniques: first-person narrative, fragmented composition, frequent allusions to contemporary events, a playful, *fantaisiste* tone undercut by moments of horror. However, the reading contract established in this book is quite different, and far more problematic. This is essentially the idea which I wish to pursue in this chapter, with particular reference to Mirbeau's blending of autobiography and fiction, to his treatment of the subject of the motor car (a novel one in 1907, obviously), and to his attempt to connect his own writing to history and historiography in a much wider sense. I also agree with Hubert Juin's judgement, expressed in his preface to the only edition of the book currently available, that *La 628–E8*, 'par son débridé et son pittoresque, par son lyrisme et sa tendresse moqueuse', is Mirbeau's masterpiece and deserves more, or more attentive, readers (*La 628–E8*, 1977: 19).

Those critics who have read Mirbeau's later works often do so in a normative way which reveals a mixture of incomprehension and hostility. Among his contemporaries, for instance, Paul Desanges characterised both *Les 21 Jours* and *La 628–E8* as 'romans', but as novels which are no more than 'des recueils de contes, ou des notes, sans autres liens que la volonté de l'auteur' (1916: 26). Similarly, Maxime Revon much preferred the play *Les Affaires sont les affaires*, written 'dans une saine tradition, à des originalités incongrues comme tels et tels romans du même écrivain' (1924: 64). More helpfully, Roland Dorgelès drew attention to the very originality which perhaps offended these critics by noting that 'Ces pamphlets romancés ne rappellent personne' (1952: 130). Hubert Juin noted too that the lack of composition of Mirbeau's books is best seen not as a clumsy fault but rather as a defining characteristic of his writing (ed. *Des artistes*, 1986: x). Reviewing an English translation of *La 628–E8* (*Sketches of a Journey*, Wilson, 1989), the historian Eugen Weber wondered whether Mirbeau's 'pleasant, undemanding account of travel through France, the Low Countries and Germany' is 'fictionalized reportage' or 'documentarized fiction' (1990: 312). (Despite my admiration for both Hubert Juin and Eugen Weber, I feel a word of warning should be added at this point. Earlier editions of *La 628–E8* are available only in major libraries and usually expurgated. Consequently it is regrettable that Juin's paperback edition of the text, though more complete, is riddled with misprints and far from reliable. As for the English translation, Weber surprisingly fails to point out in his *TLS* review that this version is both abridged and much toned down. Weber has written fascinatingly about fin-de-siècle France, and has an eye for the curious anecdote or detail not unlike Mirbeau's. Yet he underestimates Mirbeau's original book (often harrowing and far from pleasant in actual fact), and says nothing of the disappearance of half the text in a translation whose main purpose seems to be to highlight the 104 drawings by Bonnard which accompany the author's truncated words.)

One has only to read the opening pages of *La 628–E8* to perceive that this is hardly a conventional work of fiction. The dedication to Fernand Charron (the constructor of the author's automobile) is signed 'Octave Mirbeau', and the opening sentence of the text itself, with its emphatic 'donc', implies that the 'je' who is speaking is unchanged:

Voici donc le journal de ce voyage en automobile à travers un peu de la France, de la Belgique, de la Hollande, de l'Allemagne, et, surtout, à travers un peu de moi-même.
Est-ce bien un journal? Est-ce même un voyage?
N'est-ce pas plutôt des rêves, des rêveries, des souvenirs, des impressions, des récits ... (47)

Admittedly, this 'je' rarely draws attention to itself: there is no physical description or admission of social status. His profession is undeclared (journalist, dramatist, amateur explorer?). We gather that he is accompanied by a chauffeur-cum-mechanic called Charles-Louis-Eugène Brossette, whose foibles are described on several occasions; this was the name of the real chauffeur of the real *628–E8*. But who are the three other people, male and female, who leave with narrator and chauffeur 'par un beau matin d'avril 1905 [...] sur notre merveilleuse, ardente et souple C.-G.-V.' (68)? All we know is that one of them is an Englishman, Gérald B... . Mirbeau's wife, the formidable Alice Regnault, certainly does not feature in this journey of personal discovery. From time to time, the narrator fulfils his opening promise by throwing in a discreet detail about his personal life: past love affairs, frustrated pursuit of happiness, and literary success. In fact it is mainly because the narrator identifies himself as the creator of Isidore Lechat (the megalomaniac businessman hero of *Les Affaires sont les affaires*) that we are entitled to consider him to be a literary projection of Mirbeau's own personality. Leopold II, King of the

Belgians, is 'Un Lechat mieux léché' (139) (a suitably Belgian pun, perhaps); Dusseldorf industrialists possess some of Lechat's fearsome, vulgar charm (359). Reading the real world through one's own recent literary creations may be seen either as a fairly innocent sort of authorial vanity, or as a rather desperate cultural imperialism. Mirbeau cannot resist noting while passing through Krefeld that *Les Affaires sont les affaires* is on at the local theatre, although he does not bother to stop and watch the performance. His work precedes him on the journey; Mirbeau is already inscribed into history as a creator of types, as a cultural artefact himself.

In another theatre, the rudeness of German officers makes him recall an analogous confrontation with French officers in Rouen, during the Dreyfus Affair (365). Apart from the sarcastic allusion to military boorishness, Mirbeau is again laying down a modest historical marker as an active *dreyfusard* (although unfortunately his campaigning role has been overlooked by many historians of the Affair). The narrator of *La 628–E8* is certainly an avatar of Mirbeau, then, even if the promise of the opening (to travel 'à travers un peu de moi-même') leads to something other than an intimate journal. Mirbeau does not go in for self-revelation. The more gleefully he observes and exposes other people's vices, the more he conceals himself. In *La 628–E8*, the author's personality is not revealed by scanty biographical references, but by his lyricism, his humour, the novelist's visual and sensual openness to the outside world. 'Le chant des sirènes enfièvre, jusqu'au délire, ma curiosité du monde entier', he declares, in a resonant phrase evoking the Baudelairean lure of great ports (157).

What distinguishes *La 628–E8* from earlier works is that Mirbeau now becomes a direct witness of his age, dispensing with the mediation of an imaginary narrator whose fictional presence allows both author and reader to maintain a certain distance from the events narrated, to claim 'this is only a novel'. But while dismantling the fictional superstructure, he continues to cover his tracks within his story, as he indicates from the beginning. Space and time merge in this voyage. The narrator no longer distinguishes between 'la part du rêve, et [...] la part de réalité', for 'L'automobile, c'est le caprice, la fantaisie, l'incohérence' (47). Hence Hubert Juin's prefatory remark: 'Rien de rectiligne, mais des tours et des détours. Pas de plan: un désordre extrême' (30). By virtue of choosing the automobile and the genre of travel writing, perhaps the author inevitably must give pride of place to the chance encounters of the highway, to the immediacy of fleeting snapshot impressions. As he says himself, the car can be cast adrift, like a boat on water, and is freed from following the predictable parallel lines of the railway.

He also makes fun of those who freely submit to the spurious discipline of the traveller's notebook, letting Baedecker or petty bourgeois preoccupations dictate their impressions (they dutifully admire ruins and moan about the price of post cards). He intends to write 'au hasard de mes souvenirs et de mes rêves' (50). However, this hazard is less aleatory than he thinks, and Juin's 'désordre extrême' is only apparent. *La 628–E8* is a fragmentary book, but its fragments make up a coherent whole. In fact Mirbeau quotes Boileau's exhortation that 'un beau désordre soit un effet de l'art' (51). A quick glance at the table of contents reveals that the book's general structure is determined by the logic, or the logistics, of the voyage. The travellers leave France at the beginning and return at the end; geography and nationality thus largely determine their intervening circuit from Belgium to Holland, Holland to Germany, Germany to Alsace.

The narrator denies any claim to erudition or urge to communicate details, be they 'historiques, géographiques, politiques, économiques, statistiques, [...] parlementaires, édilitaires, militaires, universitaires, judiciaires' (49). This parade of suffixes suggests that it would be a mistake to take any of these branches of knowledge too seriously, or at least any taxonomic system which claimed to have mastered them. For the narrator is actually interested in everything. Innumerable pages are devoted to history, geography, economics and many other subjects. What Mirbeau dislikes are reductive abstraction and lack of irony regarding one's pretension to knowledge or eloquence. 'Toutes les phrases ne valent pas une anecdote heureuse', he remarks (354). And wherever possible, he favours what is concrete, immediate and anecdotal. Yet it would be a mistake to see *La 628–E8* as a ragbag of disconnected anecdotes. The anecdote has a paradigmatic function. For example, Mirbeau tells how Claude Monet discovered Japanese prints quite by accident in a pile of coloured paper in a shop in Zaandem; the grocer was using them as wrapping paper. This discovery triggered the evolution in French art that produced Impressionism. Hence Mirbeau's conclusion that 'L'anecdote garde, en plus de sa saveur propre, une véritable valeur historique' (220). History, or the causality of historiography, is constructed by chance, or rather by a retrospective determination of what might seem a purely aleatory chain of events. Mirbeau thus sets out to be a moralist, or rather a fabulist, in this book. In a chapter entitled 'La Faune des routes', as has been observed, he talks about the various animals encountered along the highway, moving in comic fashion from zoological observation to allegorical interpretation. This parenthesis shows Mirbeau playing the role of a La Fontaine of the automobile and takes up thirty-six pages, which might seem irrelevant to his European journey, if one did not realise that all the other episodes of the book can equally be read as fables linking the particular to the general and attempting (not always successfully) to force home a moral point. This explains the longest detour in the book, forty-five memorable pages in which the author ventures into romanced biography to recount the death of Balzac. (The account was removed from the first published edition of the book, after protests from the daughter of Balzac's widow Mme Hanska.)

* * *

Mirbeau bought his first car in 1901, the same year in which Fernand Charron and his partners Girardet and Voigt began manufacturing their own marque, the CGV. As the title itself suggests, *La 628-E8* is a celebration of the internal combustion engine and the 'bête magique', the 'fabuleuse licorne' which it drives (40–41). Remy de Gourmont was somewhat scornful of a book partly concocted from articles that had appeared in *L'Auto* (ed. Juin, 1977:23). In this he failed to grasp the social and industrial phenomenon which the motor car already represented, unlike Mirbeau himself, whose book reveals an impressive foresight akin to some of his art criticism. The historian Norman Stone has dubbed the Europe of 1900 'the classic age of Progress' (1983:15). The first decade of the twentieth century witnessed the transformation of automobilism from being a rich man's sport to a nascent mass industry, although few cheap cars were sold in France before the First World War; Charron's vehicles, for example, were still aimed at wealthy sportsmen and cost 14,000 francs each (at a time when an industrial worker or clerk might earn no more than 2,000 francs a year). Many of the early enthusiasts were aristocrats of right-wing views, such as the Marquis de Dion, founder of the Automobile Club de France (1895), rally organiser, manufacturer, backer of the daily

L'Auto, and violent anti-*dreyfusard*; he was arrested for assaulting President Loubet at the Auteuil races in 1899. (See Laux, 1976; Overy, 1990; Weber, 1986.) Mirbeau himself thus exemplifies an intermediate stage in the transition from élitist sport to an ever-widening middle-class market, a process of democratisation which has been related to 'corresponding political shifts towards mass politics and greater equality' (Overy, 1990: 62). There were about 21,000 motor-driven vehicles in France in 1906, and over 90,000 in 1913 (whereas there were over one million in the USA just before the War). France was the first home of the automobile industry, although it was overtaken in production by the USA in 1904–05. At the turn of the century, demand vastly exceeded production in France, which amounted to only 400 cars in 1897, rising twenty or thirtyfold however by 1901 and 1902. The narrator of *La 628–E8* sketches in the economic consequences of this rapid development from artisanal specialisation to large-scale distribution, noting that the heroic age of the first automobiles, where the restrictions of a luxury market allowed the shameless exploitation of wealthy, ignorant clients and profits of 1,000 percent, is now gone. The constant refrain uttered by the chauffeur Brossette as a means of justifying his illicit gains at his master's expense ('Tout ça, c'est des histoires de riches' (59,61,67)), will soon be a thing of the past.

On 30 August 1910, while driving in the *628–E8* between Paris and Nanterre, Mirbeau knocked down a cyclist, who was 'fortement contusionné', according to the dossier kept in the Paris Préfecture de police (B.A.1190). (Ten years earlier, Gide's wife had been run over by a car on the Place de la Concorde and suffered two broken arms.) As we know only too well, the motor car is both means of escape and means of destruction. Intercity races, held on the open road, began in Europe in 1895 with Paris-Bordeaux-Paris. 'They were bloody spectacles' (Flink, 1988: 31), forbidden in Britain and the USA. In the 1903 Paris-Madrid-Paris race, most of the competitors' vehicles were capable of reaching speeds of 140 kms per hour. Newspaper accounts of the race reveal that five drivers were killed (including the brother of Louis Renault), as well as a similar number of spectators. Unsurprisingly, Rochefort's *L'Intransigeant* wrote of 'massacres organisés', while Léon Daudet in *Le Gaulois* demanded a complete ban on races or better still of motorised vehicles altogether (Sapin, 1966: 148). 'Thenceforward, intercity races in Europe were run on closed circuits' (Flink, 1988: 31). Certain left-wing municipalities sometimes imposed speed limits of six miles per hour on motorists; those who broke the general limit of 30 kms per hour might occasionally find themselves in prison. But the Marquis de Dion considered the motor car's forward rush to be inexorable: 'L'avenir de l'automobile est plus important que nos vies. Rien ne peut arrêter le progrès, mais il exige beaucoup de sacrifices' (Sapin, 1966: 176).

In these circumstances, it is easier to understand why Mirbeau describes automobilism as 'une maladie mentale', the main symptom of which is speed (*628–E8*, 51). Speed is 'névropathique', a 'mal d'être ailleurs, sans cesse ailleurs, plus loin qu'ailleurs'. The brain becomes 'une piste sans fin où pensées, images, sensations ronflent et roulent, à raison de cent kilomètres à l'heure' (51). Everyday life is 'animée d'un mouvement fou', in a 'sensation douloureuse, parfois, mais forte, fantastique et grisante, comme le vertige et comme la fièvre' (52). The narrator of *Les 21 Jours d'un neurasthénique* sought out originals and madmen as an oasis of freedom in the desert of bourgeois servility (332); this is what makes Mirbeau's writing simultaneously appealing, provocative and grotesque. In *La 628–E8*, the car offers a new-found freedom, where the frontiers of space seemingly replace those of social norms; but again, this liberty is inherently dangerous, and the prerogative of a privileged élite.

In the dedication of *La 628–E8*, the narrator offers a fairly wide definition of this liberty, metaphysical as much as physical. In his automobile, he is carried not simply across space, but also 'à travers des mœurs cachées, des idées en travail, à travers de l'histoire, notre histoire vivante d'aujourd'hui' (37). The car 'est ma vie, ma vie artistique et spirituelle, autant et plus que ma maison' (or his books and paintings), for these latter objects remain fixed in a death-like immobility (40). Moreover, the machine exemplifies human genius and imagination far more powerfully than works conventionally recognised as specimens of high art; technology should not be excluded from the aesthetic perspective of critics and newspapers.

Yet such vertiginous sensations of freedom from spatial, sensual or aesthetic norms are reserved for an élite. One cannot help feeling that their intensity is determined not merely by their novelty but by this exclusiveness. Many of the satirical jibes in *La 628–E8* are directed at familiar targets, with the author's customary caricatural verve. Mirbeau's stance is superficially libertarian and anti-bourgeois. Thus in a hotel in Givet, the narrator catches sight of a grotesquely ugly middle-class family (such specimens already swarm through the pages of *Les 21 Jours*); 'famille bien française', as he concludes with sarcastic relish. (It is worth noting parenthetically that the vehement protestations uttered by angry Belgians who were unflattered by Mirbeau's portrait of them in his book failed to take account of his caustic treatment of his own compatriots.) In any case, Mirbeau cannot tolerate the idea of these charmless bourgeois, who are the proprietors of a jam factory and stew in the juices of their imbecility, partaking in the delights of automobilism. Their Brulard-Taponnier breaks down and they are forced to take the train. Later the chauffeur Brossette tells the narrator that there was nothing actually wrong with their car: they had been swindled by their wily mechanic who was reluctant to leave his flighty wife unattended.

Unsurprisingly, Mirbeau similarly seeks to exclude much of Belgium from the automobilist élite; like many of his compatriots, he regards this country as inherently derisory. Brussels is a city which is 'complètement parodique' (89), and so the 'engins formidables' circulating in the streets prove on closer inspection to be cardboard tigers. Searching under the enormous hood of one of these mighty monsters, the narrator finally unearths a 'minuscule mécanisme, monocylindrique, de la grosseur d'une tasse à café chinoise, et dont la force ne doit pas excéder un cheval et demi' (98). A perfect symbol of the pretentiousness and impotence of the natives of Brussels; indeed, the driver cannot even manage to get his tiny engine started. Such mechanical and aesthetic dysfunction is the negative version of Mirbeau's futuristic reflections on the motor car as harbinger of progress and freedom.

The sacrifices which the Marquis de Dion observed were required by progress clearly fascinate Mirbeau. In the midst of a chapter on 'La Faune des routes' (many specimens of which end up bloodily under his wheels), the narrator indulges in a piece of humanitarian rhetoric, as a sort of counterpoint to some of the excesses of his book. Unlike 'les hommes du pouvoir',

j'ai grand pitié du malheur humain. [...] je suis, moi, aveuglément aussi, et toujours, avec le pauvre contre le riche, avec l'assommé contre l'assommeur, avec le malade contre la maladie [...] je n'entends rien aux subtilités de la politique. Et elles me blessent comme une injustice. (303)

However, he admits that the intoxication of automobilism obliterates such well-intentioned sentiments and replaces them with a 'mégalomanie cosmogonique' (304). A driver whose car has just run over a peasant girl pronounces a Panglossian speech in favour of progress which takes the Marquis de Dion's views to parodic extremes, as he demonstrates that the car driver is working not merely for industry but for 'le bonheur universel' (307). It may seem that those who fall by the wayside of progress occasionally take their revenge: for example, Baron von B... is ordered to pay 1,200 francs compensation to a girl who stumbled under the wheels of his car, although she was uninjured (326). Yet such an episode really illustrates the theme of conflict, exploitation and brutality which recurs throughout Mirbeau's journey and which suggests his utterances about solidarity are no more than pious hopes.

Even if Mirbeau claims that the subtleties of politics both escape and offend him, he is clearly fascinated by systems of government and their influence (usually nefarious) on the individual citizen. Several crowned heads make their appearance in *La 628–E8*, from Louis XIV to Léopold II and Wilhelm II. There can be no doubt too that he is even more fascinated and offended by the suffering and injustice which afflict the anonymous mass of people deprived of political power than by the double-dealing of governments. Certain episodes are clearly inserted in the book with the intention of raising such issues, and need to be read in a different, more literal way from other pages where the author's penchant for black humour and the macabre distance us from his subject matter. Nevertheless, Mirbeau's position always remains equivocal, even, or perhaps especially, when he writes in denunciatory mode: not only is he a wealthy member of the social class which is the prime beneficiary of the excesses he deplores, but by writing about suffering and exploitation he is also creating an uncomfortable sadomasochistic complicity with the reader.

Mirbeau makes frequent references to colonialism and its economic effects throughout the book. The cheese merchants of Purnerend call their cheeses, which are shaped like red or violaceous balls, 'têtes de nègres', and heap them up in pyramids or use them for juggling. From a distance, it seems that 'ils jouent à la balle, avec leurs propres têtes' (263). The wheel of the *628–E8* makes violent contact with one of these flying balls and turns it into 'un peu de pâte rouge, aplatie' (264). This incident would be a trivial one, were it not that the metaphor of the negroes' head recalled more sinister episodes. In 'Prostitution', the narrator remembers the Rideck (the red-light district of Antwerp) of thirty years before, a sort of colonial exhibition where flesh of every colour could be purchased. In particular, he recalls a negress from Dahomey, lying naked on a yellow silk mattress and recounting to him the splendours of her country, such as the King's palace, the roof of which was made of severed heads skilfully arranged like a mosaic. To stop the rain leaking through this flimsy covering, the heads need to be replaced on a regular basis, so that the ground is continually soaked crimson by blood. And 'l'aspect en est vraiment féerique [...] et l'odeur délicieuse' (193), just like the flying cheeses with their 'odeur aigrelette' which form part of 'une opérette féerique' (263).

Such passages are a dubious mixture of cultural relativism, black humour, and complaisant denunciation of atrocities, and remind us evidently of *Le Jardin des supplices*, that voyage to the end of a malodorous Oriental fairyland. The atrocities of the Dahomean charnel-houses or the Chinese torture garden exist outside the colonial system, which grants them a macabre, innovative charm, as far as Mirbeau's narrators are concerned. In other cases, however, the author avoids the sadistic facility of this anecdote. Passing by a small shop in Belgium, his eye is caught by another pyramid, made this time from small samples of rubber. His imagination rapidly moves from this harmless shop window to scenes from the land of this 'caoutchouc rouge', the Belgian Congo. Once again, he thinks of the 'féeries de ce paradis', of its inhabitants, those 'nègres puérils', whose untamed innocence makes them like children or even rabbits (147). (Mirbeau shares the anthropological prejudices of his age about racial differences, whatever his contempt for supposed colonialist supremacy.) This pacific vision is disrupted by the arrival of trafficker, colonist and functionary, accompanied by executions, massacres and tortures; the trees are slashed apart, as are 'les déplorables races indigènes'; if the rubber runs short, a dozen heads are sent bouncing between the huts (149).

This bloody reverie (the worst images are unpleasantly sadistic and have not been cited here) contains nevertheless a moral point, which actually acquires for the modern reader an anachronistic force greater than it probably had in the days of fin-de-siècle Empire. Mirbeau encapsulates his message rather tellingly in the phrase 'du sang nègre poisse à tous nos pneus' (149). This epigram is equivalent to the famous riposte made by the mutilated slave in Voltaire's *Candide*: his missing limbs are the price paid for eating sugar in Europe. The intention is both to establish a causality which the colonisers would prefer to conceal or deny, and to draw the reader himself into this chain of cause and effect. All Western consumers are made responsible for this system of exploitation which stems from the association of 'les races inférieures à notre civilisation' (149). The atrocities committed by administrators in the Belgian Congo had in fact been well documented: for example in a parliamentary report published in 1904 by Roger Casement. Joseph Conrad described this venture as 'the vilest scramble for loot that ever disfigured the history of human conscience' (cited in *Heart of Darkness*, 1990: xxi). On leaving the shop, the narrator of *La 628-E8* is also offered ivory; but that is a story Mirbeau was not prescient enough to explore.

Sometimes, members of these inferior races venture as far as Europe, like the prostitute or 'deux pauvres nègres, en habit noir, chapeau de haute forme' (173), seen singing and dancing a lament for their homeland on the quays in Antwerp. By dressing them in this derisory, European capitalist's uniform, Mirbeau is evidently continuing his critique of the dubious benefits of civilisation. (D.B. Tubbs, the English translator of *La 628-E8*, chose to excise the entire episode dealing with atrocities in the Congo. The quayside scene in Antwerp, 'Minstrels', is retained, but the omission of the words 'deux pauvres nègres' has the unfortunate effect of making the passage read like a patronising, racially stereotyped presentation of exotic characters.) However, it is the narrator's encounter with another exile which produces one of the most powerful sections of the book, entitled 'Pogromes'.

The narrator is observing impoverished emigrants embarking for America. The most destitute are the Jews, who drag along their 'affreux boulet d'infamie' (176). Although Mirbeau has long since renounced the explicit anti-Semitism of his early writing, such phrases remind us how equivocal his ideological position often is in practice, whatever his flirtation with anarchism. Wealthy Jews in fact still form part of his demonology: thus 'le juif pauvre paie pour le juif riche' (176), for the conqueror who himself becomes 'le complice et, le plus souvent, le trésorier de toutes les réactions, même de la réaction antisémite' (177). Luckily, the narrator prefers to shelve this dangerous line of argument in order to present the account, or the parable, of an old Russian Jew, a new Job who expresses 'toute la fatigue du malheur humain' (178). With his long beard, his drooling lips and his foul breath, this accursed figure is a latter-day ancient mariner, who detains the passing traveller in order to tell him a tale of unspeakable woe. However, on this occasion, Mirbeau resists the temptation of embroidering in horrific or comic mode on the atrocious events which are related. The Jew has been expelled from everywhere, stripped of everything, and had all the members of his family massacred one after the other in the revolutionary upheavals of the new century. (Waves of pogroms in 1903 and 1905 brought the deaths of hundreds and the ruin of thousands; the public disorder which caused them was often instigated by the tsarist regime, in a grim foretaste of the systematic massacres which would follow during the Russian civil war (Baron, 1987).) How does one react faced with 'cette invraisemblable accumulation de crime' (184), and this eternal victim of human malevolence? Tears do not suffice. The narrator admits to being numbed, paralysed, 'saturé d'horreur', and turns away from the old Jew, who in any case 'ne me demandait rien que de me taire' (189).

Mirbeau is in effect posing the question, half a century early, of Holocaust literature. Does silence represent failure, a creative impasse, or rather an affirmation of human dignity? He never claimed to be able to resolve this problem, which is perhaps insoluble. With a rather facile optimism, he wrote in 1895 that

> aujourd'hui l'action doit se réfugier dans le livre. C'est dans le livre seul, que, dégagée des contingences malsaines et multiples qui l'annihilent et l'étouffent, elle peut trouver le terrain propre à la germination des idées qu'elle sème. (*Les Écrivains*, II, 1926: 27)

Five years later, however, Mirbeau retreated from this position which is curiously close to Mallarmean symbolism. In the meantime, he had chosen to engage himself in the 'contingences malsaines' of the Dreyfus Affair. Despite his choice of the 'right' side, he saw in the second condemnation of 1899 and the ensuing amnesty of 1900 (which absolved guilty and innocent alike) the impossibility of attaining truth or justice, and wrote more pessimistically: 'L'idée dort dans les livres ... La vérité et le bonheur n'en sortent jamais' (*Combats pour l'enfant*, 1990: 200). In our own era of revisionism, of left or right, we can at least claim that writing has the function of bearing witness. A non-conformist writer like Mirbeau is both journalist and witness, a chronicler of everyday history who sets out to unmask the lies of officialdom, even if the new truth which he serves up may strike some readers to be as perverted as the old one.

In actual fact, the author of *La 628–E8* clearly announces his intention of modifying the interpretations of traditional history. Thus he has Baron von B... remark, when talking of Bismarck and German emperors, that 'toute l'histoire est à refaire' (333). He has already applied this observation to the age of Louis XIV, the so-called great century. Unlike the academies, 'gardiennes sévères des mensonges du passé', he compares favourably the 'vertueux hauts-de-forme' and 'honnêtes habits noirs' of modern politicians, with their modest venality and their 'petits Panamas', to the 'siècle abominable' of Louis XIV, that 'règne monstrueux et fétide, dont l'odeur de latrines, de bordel, vous prend à la gorge, et vous fait tourner, soulever le cœur, jusqu'au vomissement!' (77–79).

These hygienic reflections typify the scatological humour favoured by Mirbeau and some of his contemporaries. The modern Western reader, protected from certain realities by mains drainage, pure water and public health provision, may be inclined to dismiss them as essentially trivial attempts at taboo-breaking. Yet as Eugen Weber reminds us, in 1900 'Few French of any class came close to comfort as we conceive it today' (1986: 186). Direct drainage to the sewers was little developed outside Paris; even within Paris, only one house in ten was connected to the system. The supposedly grand hotels frequented by Proust boasted more elevators than water closets; regular washing, of bodies or clothes, was a difficult and rare business. Mirbeau's materialistic interpretation of history as a lesson in hygiene is thus less of a caricature than might be thought. The French take pride in their filth, a 'tare héréditaire': 'Malpropreté monarchique et catholique à qui Louis XIV donna le caractère d'une vertu, et la force d'émulation d'un concours' (321). Mirbeau cites Chamfort's anecdote of a nobleman who ordered his servants to piss liberally over the approaches to his château, in an attempt to emulate the urinary odours of Versailles. This is no doubt one of the reasons why Mirbeau finds in Jarry's faecal Ubu 'l'image la plus parfaite qu'on nous ait encore donnée des Empereurs, des Rois' (350). A hotelier complains that twentieth-century Frenchmen still have not learned how to shit properly: confronted with an English water-closet, 'ils montent toujours dessus' (322). (This observation is paralleled by a court case cited by Weber, where a man balancing in this position broke the seat, fell and fractured an arm, and promptly sued the owner of the casino where the accident took place.) As Weber remarks, 'The shift from squatting to sitting to defecate was surely as difficult to negotiate as the shift from coins to paper money' (1986: 186–87).

Mirbeau's confrontation with bodily functions is however more than a matter of satirical jibes deriving from his observation of how technological progress (whether water closets or motor cars) modifies everyday history. At the beginning of *La 628–E8*, he enumerates the bodily organs which govern his humour or humours, noting that 'Ce que M. Paul Bourget appelle des «états de l'esprit», ce n'est jamais que des «états de la matière»' (50); and he adds, 'Loin de m'en plaindre, je m'en réjouis' (51). A metaphysic which might be summed up, then, as 'Je pense donc je chie' (or vice versa). Nevertheless, his claim that he rejoices in this is a surprising one, even if we bear in mind the fact that Mirbeau made contradiction one of his guiding principles (producing a famous self-justifying article on this topic called 'Palinodies!' in 1898). Contradiction itself is actually reduced to physiological causes: 'Selon que mes organes fonctionnent bien ou mal, il m'arrive de détester, aujourd'hui, ce que j'aimais hier' (51). Be that as it may, his reverie on the miasmas fermenting at the bottom of the polluted canals in Amsterdam is far more typical of his entropic vision (to use Baguley's phrase (1990)) of the human and social body. Fate or evolution decree that our vital organs are 'une infection et une honte' (262). A direct apostrophe follows:

> Lecteur, le divin Platon allait chaque jour à la selle, ignoblement, comme il faut qu'y aille, chaque jour, ta bien-aimée. Si elle n'y va pas pas, le cher cœ ur, elle ne t'aimera plus ... Constipé, le divin Platon devient aussitôt une brute quinteuse et stupide. L'intestin commande au cerveau ... Quant à cette putréfaction que les villes font sous elles, elle menace toutes les agglomérations, à la façon, songes-y bien, dont les ordures sociales et les reliefs du plaisir des riches menacent les sociétés d'une fermentation inapaisable de la misère. (262)

Here we find, barely concealed by the sarcastic tone, that sense of the curse of the flesh which haunts both the work of Mirbeau himself and that of much of the decadent literature of his age. The bowel moves the brain, and the brute the philosopher; the evolutionary cycle is bound to a regressive, atavistic determinism. Mirbeau and his contemporaries as it were make scatology into eschatology (the most striking example is Huysmans' exercise in post-naturalist hagiography, *Sainte Lydwine de Schiedam* (1901), where putrescent flesh is re-inscribed into Christian myth). It can indeed be observed that this perception of the body is a Christian one, where the prospect of grace or redemption has been removed, for as Noëlle Châtelet writes

> Le corps, dans la hiérarchie chrétienne, vit la chute au travers d'une fatalité biologique où menstrues, sperme, selles, urine, sueur, larmes confluent en un flot de bourbe avilissante. (1977: 54)

In Mirbeau's reverie, note too how we pass from the shameful individual body to the collective putrefaction which spreads throughout the social body and threatens its integrity. That being said, it is unclear whether the 'fermentation inapaisable de la misère' stands for the revolutionary potential of the dispossessed or simply the stench of injustice; the likely cause or course of Mirbeau's excremental apocalypse is somewhat ambiguous.

To conclude these comments on Mirbeau's journey around Europe, technology and ontogeny, it seems appropriate to look at one of his own closing passages, the notorious account of Balzac's death, where once again he treats the relationship of the literary imagination to the forces of history and biology in his inimitable (and to some, highly offensive) fashion. The narrator characterises his own imagination as 'ardente, féroce, carnassière' (375), and so naturally is drawn to the work of Balzac, which he describes in adjectives which could be a self-portrait as 'si subversive, si dissolvante, si immorale' (378). The Balzac of *La 628–E8*, however, is a sensual being, as much body as creative genius. Although he was apparently 'parcimonieusement armé pour l'amour' (372), he displayed a 'gourmandise pantagruélique'. Just as when eating a peach, 'le jus lui en coulait partout' (379), so too enormous drops of fetid sweat stream down his body and inundate his deathbed (406). It proved impossible to make a death mask of the deceased writer, for 'Le nez avait entièrement coulé sur le drap' (415). However, unlike the 'divine Plato', the great Balzac maintains his spiritual integrity to the last, even when betrayed by his future widow, who is already consoling herself with her lover. 'Au milieu de la putréfaction de ses organes, le cerveau demeurait sain, intact. L'imagination y régnait en souveraine immaculée' (400). The case of Balzac is doubly exemplary: it illustrates both that physiological fatality which frequently takes the form of liquefaction and deliquescence in Mirbeau's work, and the possibility of redemption, of an inscription into history which is reserved for the elect.

Other solutions to physical and political corruption are fleetingly envisaged. From time to time, Mirbeau flirts with eugenics as another means of revitalising the race. Fortunately, perhaps, the subject is normally a vehicle for burlesque comedy. For example, the Belgians have fabricated a breed of rabbit grandiosely known as 'le géant des Flandres' (133). (In Bonnard's drawing which accompanies an illustrated edition of the book, this super-rabbit is the same size as a young elephant.) A hen-breeder promotes incest as the 'seul moyen de reconstituer une race dégénérée' (135), but finally admits to the narrator that the racial superiority of his fowls has more to do with skilful faking than with the laws of genetics. Consequently, the method is unlikely to work for the Belgians themselves, a bastardised amalgam of inferior races compared unfavourably to the racial superiority of the Germans (84, 99, 418).

Inevitably, perhaps, Mirbeau shares some of the prejudices and obsessions of his age concerning racial and sexual degeneration (thus the narrator observes a French youth whom he deems to be manifestly 'aveuli par des habitudes solitaires' (83)). Such attitudes distance us from him, of course, but do not necessarily diminish the force of his social criticism or the documentary and literary value of his book. Like the hens and the Belgians, Mirbeau has himself created in *La 628-E8* a bastardised genre, which straddles fiction, autobiography and travel writing and allows him to put down a historical marker as a literary innovator. This generic equivocation is equally matched by his ideological equivocations and double-edged humour, where humanitarian outrage and morbid delectation mingle uneasily. Mirbeau's voyage in *La 628-E8* should inspire modern readers as much as his contemporaries to take a ticket to ride, if not to become fellow travellers.

Conclusion

Octave Mirbeau died on 16 February 1917, his sixty-ninth birthday. During his final years, he grew a long white beard, in the fashion of a Tolstoyan patriarch, but otherwise sank into a protracted physical and mental decline, publishing almost nothing after *Dingo* in 1913. This is one reason why the authorship of his supposedly final piece of writing is bitterly contested: that is, the 'Testament politique d'Octave Mirbeau', which appeared in *Le Petit Parisien* on 19 February 1917. Was the dying author actually intellectually capable of composing or dictating his final thoughts? Their edifying banality is, moreover, quite untypical of the writer's previous libertarian provocations; as the mechanised slaughter of the Great War grinds relentlessly on, he denounces German aggression and asserts that 'l'humanité sera régénérée par la France' (*Combats politiques*, 268). But we may well ask, in a wider sense, what legacy he left us. Whatever his anarchist evangelising, as a literary creator Mirbeau manifestly has none of Tolstoy's imaginative range and energy; it is an absurd presumption to thrust him into the ranks of the major nineteenth-century European novelists. Apart from anything else, from a purely quantitative point of view, too much of Mirbeau's writing was ephemeral journalism. The dozen or so books which survive belong to the category of post-naturalist decadence, whose thematics and poetics have been effectively defined by commentators like Jennifer Birkett (1986). Nonetheless, while he shares the morbid, sadomasochistic obsession with degeneration of so many of his contemporaries, Mirbeau does escape the fusty solemnity and posturing mannerism which now cling to turn-of-the-century writers like Gourmont, Péladan or Lorrain and which make reading their texts a painful exercise in literary exhumation.

As we have seen, Mirbeau himself was mercilessly aware of his own limitations as a creative artist; the honesty of his judgement should not be overlooked. Predictable, repetitive rhetoric certainly features in his books (especially if one extends the corpus to include the early hack works discovered by Pierre Michel). Yet there are also many fiery pages where his writing shines with a brighter image: provocation, perversity, macabre humour, bizarre inventions allied to satirical jibes at figures and abuses of the Belle Epoque. Sylvie Thiéblemont concludes her biography of Mirbeau with the observation that he is 'un personnage indéfinissable' (1986: 332). He remains indeed a paradoxical and intangible writer. His early novels may be of autobiographical inspiration, yet there is no real introspection in them. His personal life remains a mystery, if one renounces the facile urge to read fictional rhetoric as a direct expression of real character traits. (It is regrettable, in this respect, that so much of his correspondence remains unpublished.) Paradoxical too is the alternation between violence and compassion, cynicism and sentimentality, preaching and irony which typifies his writing. As a public figure, he escaped the prosecution and persecution inflicted on anarchists like Jean Grave or committed *dreyfusards* like Zola, although he was vociferously present at their side. Conflict, social, natural or individual, recurs throughout his books; there are moments of lyrical intensity and resignation, but rarely of serenity or quietude. Mirbeau was too conscious of personal agony and collective atrocity to be anything other than a sardonic pessimist. We now look back at what we call the Belle Epoque with a certain fond nostalgia, for the scandals and injustices which aroused Mirbeau's indignation were subsequently dwarfed by the annihilative inventiveness of the later twentieth century. Mirbeau saw evil in humanity, society and nature and found no doctrine adequate to explain or eradicate its insidious presence; in this sense, he remains a writer for our times. And above all, we should value him, not simply as a creator of memorable grotesques or as a master of polemical verve, but also as a compelling, open-minded witness to his own time, to that age which vanished in the cataclysm of the Great War and whose aesthetics his work captures so tellingly. No Tolstoy, then, yet an innovative chronicler who merits his place alongside Huysmans, Maupassant or Apollinaire in the fin-de-siècle pantheon.

Bibliography

The following bibliography lists only those works cited and consulted in the preparation of this study. Readers seeking more exhaustive bibliographical information on writings by and about Octave Mirbeau are advised to consult P. Michel and J.-F. Nivet, *Octave Mirbeau* (1990), which is complemented by J.-F. Nivet's doctoral thesis (1987) and the annual *Cahiers Octave Mirbeau* (numbers for 1994 and 1995 published to date). Place of publication is Paris and London for works in French and English, unless otherwise indicated.

WORKS BY MIRBEAU

Le Comédien. Réponse à M. Mirbeau (Brunox, 1883)
Le Salon de 1885 (Baschet, 1885)
Lettres de ma chaumière (Laurent, 1886)
Le Calvaire (Ollendorff, 1886; UGE, 10/18, 1986, preface by H. Juin)
L'Abbé Jules (Ollendorff, 1888; UGE, 10/18, 1977, preface by H. Juin)
Sébastien Roch (Charpentier, 1890; UGE, 10/18, 1977, preface by H. Juin)
Contes de la chaumière (Charpentier/Fasquelle, 1894; Editions le Goût de l'Etre, 1987, introduction by T. Maricourt)
Le Jardin des supplices (Fasquelle, 1899; Gallimard, Folio, 1988, ed. M. Delon)
Le Journal d'une femme de chambre (Fasquelle, 1900; Flammarion, GF, 1983, preface by M. Mercier; Gallimard, Folio, 1984, ed. N. Arnaud; Le Livre de poche, 1986, preface by L. Bodard, notes by D. Leuwers)
Les 21 Jours d'un neurasthénique (Fasquelle, 1901; UGE, 10/18, 1977, preface by H. Juin; Editions de Septembre, 1990, preface by R. Fouano)
La 628-E8 (Fasquelle, 1907; UGE, 10/18, 1977, preface by H. Juin)
Dingo (Fasquelle, 1913; Editions de Maule, 1987)
La Vache tachetée (Flammarion, 1918)
Chez l'illustre écrivain (Flammarion, 1919)
La Pipe de cidre (Flammarion, 1919)
Un gentilhomme (Flammarion, 1920)

Théâtre, I (Flammarion, 1921; contains *Vieux ménage, Les Affaires sont les affaires, L'Epidémie*)
Théâtre, II (Flammarion, 1921; contains *Interview, Le Portefeuille, Les Mauvais Bergers, Scrupules*)
Théâtre, III (Flammarion, 1922; contains *Le Foyer, Les Amants*)
Des artistes, 2 vols (Flammarion, 1922 &1924; UGE, 10/18, 1986, preface by H. Juin)
Gens de théâtre (Flammarion, 1924)
Les Ecrivains, 2 vols (Flammarion, 1925 & 1926)
Les Grimaces et quelques autres chroniques (Flammarion, 1927)
Correspondance avec Auguste Rodin (Tusson, Du Lérot, 1988, ed. P. Michel & J.-F. Nivet)
Dans le ciel (Caen, L'Echoppe, 1989, ed. P. Michel & J.-F. Nivet)
Lettres à Alfred Bansard des Bois (Montpellier, Editions du Limon, 1989, ed P. Michel)
Combats politiques (Séguier, 1990, ed. P. Michel & J.-F. Nivet)
Combats pour l'enfant (Vauchrétien, Ivan Davy, 1990, ed. P. Michel)
Contes cruels, 2 vols (Séguier, 1990, ed. P. Michel & J.-F. Nivet)
Correspondance avec Camille Pissarro (Tusson, Du Lérot, 1990, ed. P. Michel & J.-F. Nivet)
Correspondance avec Claude Monet (Tusson, Du Lérot, 1990, ed. P. Michel & J.-F. Nivet)
Notes sur l'art (Caen, L'Echoppe, 1990, ed. J.-F. Nivet & P. Michel)
L'Affaire Dreyfus (Séguier, 1991, ed. P. Michel & J.-F. Nivet)
Lettres de l'Inde (Caen, L'Echoppe, 1991, ed. P. Michel & J.-F. Nivet)
Sac au dos (Caen, L'Echoppe, 1991, ed. J.-F. Nivet & P. Michel)
Combats esthétiques, 2 vols (Séguier, 1993, ed. P. Michel & J.-F. Nivet)
Croquis bretons (Rezé, Séquences, 1993, ed. J.-F. Nivet)
Veuve. Paysage de foule (Alfil, 1993)
L'Amour de la femme vénale (Indigo & Côté-femmes, 1994, translated from Bulgarian by A. Lévy, preface by A. Corbin, notes by P. Michel)

Correspondance générale (a multi-volume edition edited by Michel and Nivet was announced in 1993, but publication has been delayed for copyright reasons)

OTHER WORKS CONSULTED

Apter, E.S., 'Fétichisme et domesticité: Freud, Mirbeau, Buñuel', *Poétique*, 70 (1987), 143–66
Aron, J.-P., ed., *Misérable et glorieuse: la femme du XIXe siècle* (Fayard, 1980)
L'Avant-scène cinéma, 36 (1964) [on Buñuel's film of *Le Journal d'une femme de chambre*]
L'Avant-scène théâtre, 706 (1982) [on Jacques Destoop's stage production of *Le Journal d'une femme de chambre*]
Aymé, M., *Les Contes du chat perché* (Gallimard, Folio, 1975)
Baguley, D., *Naturalist Fiction: the entropic vision* (Cambridge UP, 1990)
Barnes, J., *Flaubert's Parrot* (Cape, 1984)
Baron, S.W., *The Russian Jew under Tsars and Soviets*, 2nd edition (New York, Schocken, 1987)
Baudelaire, C., *Œuvres complètes* (Seuil, L'Intégrale, 1968)
Bauquenne, A., *La Maréchale*, 4th edition, preface by A. Daudet (Ollendorff, 1883)
———, *Ménages parisiens*, 4th edition (Ollendorff, 1883)
———, *La Belle Madame Le Vassart* (Ollendorff, 1884)
———, *Amours cocasses* (Ollendorff, 1885) [Reprinted with *Ménages parisiens* (Nizet, 1995), ed. P. Michel, and attributed to Mirbeau]
Beer, G., *Darwin's Plots: evolutionary narrative in Darwin, George Eliot and nineteenth-century fiction* (RKP, 1983)
Bergson, H., *Le Rire: essai sur la signification du comique* (Alcan, 1927)
Berlin, I., *The Hedgehog and the Fox* (Weidenfeld & Nicolson, 1953)
Binder, H., *Kafka Kommentar zu sämtlichen Erzählungen* (Munich, Winkler, 1975)
Birkett, J., *The Sins of the Fathers: decadence in France 1870–1914* (Quartet Books, 1986)
Bourget, P., *Le Disciple* (Nelson, n.d.)
———, *Essais de psychologie contemporaine* (Plon, 1899)
Brush, S.G., *The Temperature of History: phases of science and culture in the nineteenth century* (New York, Franklin, 1978)
Burns, W., '"In the Penal Colony": variations on a theme by Octave Mirbeau', *Accent*, 17 (1957), 45–51

Busby, K., ed., *Correspondances: studies in literature, history and the arts in nineteenth-century France* (Amsterdam, Rodopi, 1992)
Les Cahiers d'aujourd'hui, 9 (1922) [pp.101–80 on Mirbeau]
Les Cahiers naturalistes, 64 (1990) [dossier Octave Mirbeau, 7–102]
Cahiers Octave Mirbeau, 1 (1994–)
Carr, R., *Anarchism in France: the case of Octave Mirbeau* (Manchester UP, 1977)
Carrière, J.-C., ed., *Anthologie de l'humour noir 1900* (Les Editions 1900, 1988)
Chaine, P., *Le Jardin des supplices: pièce en trois tableaux, d'après le roman d'Octave Mirbeau* (Librairie théâtrale, 1929)
Châtelet, N., *Le Corps à corps culinaire* (Seuil, 1977)
Chen, P.M., *Law and Justice: the legal system in China 2400 B.C. to 1960 A.D.* (Dunellen Publishing Company, 1973)
Cogny, P., 'Octave Mirbeau et Félicien Rops: quelques lettres inédites', *Les Cahiers naturalistes*, 16 (1960), 619–24
Colloque Octave Mirbeau, ed. P. Michel (Les Editions du Demi-Cercle, 1994)
Conrad, J., *Heart of Darkness and Other Tales*, ed. C. Watts (OUP, 1990)
Cronin, V., *Paris on the Eve 1900–1914* (Collins, 1989)
Curtis, M., *Three against the Third Republic: Sorel, Barrès and Maurras* (Princeton UP, 1959)
Darragon, E., 'L'Œil Mirbeau'*Critique*, 558 (1993), 739–51
Darien, G., *Le Voleur* (UGE, 10/18, 1971)
Darwin, C., *The Illustrated Origin of Species*, ed. R. Leakey (Faber & Faber, 1979)
Defays, J.-M., 'Mystification et démystification chez Alphonse Allais', *French Studies*, 45 (1991), 279–94
Desanges, P., *Octave Mirbeau* (Librairie d'action d'art de la ghilde «Les Forgerons», 1916)
Dorgelès, R., *Portraits sans retouche* (Albin Michel, 1952)
Eisenzweg, U., 'Le Capitaine et la femme de chambre: l'affaire Dreyfus et la crise de la vérité narrative', *Romantisme*, 84 (1994), 79–92
Flaubert, G., *Correspondance*, vols 1 & 2, ed. J. Bruneau (Gallimard, Pléiade, 1973 & 1980)
Flink, J.J., *The Automobile Age* (Cambridge, Mass., MIT Press, 1988)
Forsan, *Dans la vieille rue* (Ollendorff, 1885)

Foucault, M., *Discipline and Punish: the birth of the prison*, trans. A. Sheridan (Allen Lane, 1977)
Fournel, *Les Artistes français contemporains* (Tours, Alfred Mame, 1884)
Fournier, A., 'Parterres et châteaux de Mirbeau', *Europe*, 458 (1967), 191–212
Fox, M.W., ed., *The Wild Canids* (New York, Van Nostrand Reinhold, 1975)
Freud, S., *Jokes and their Relation to the Unconscious*, trans./ed. J. Strachey (RKP, 1966)
Genet, J., *Le Balcon* (Gallimard, Folio, 1979)
Gide, A., *Journal*, 2 vols (Gallimard, Pléiade, 1951 & 1954)
Gobin, P., 'Un code des postures dans les romans de Mirbeau?', in *La Lecture sociocritique du texte romanesque*, ed. G. Falconer & H. Mitterand (Toronto, Hakkert, 1975), 189–206
Gombrich, E.H., *Art and Illusion: a study in the psychology of pictorial representation*, 5th edition (Phaidon, 1977)
Goncourt, E. & J. de, *Journal*, 3 vols, ed. R. Ricatte (Laffont, Bouquins, 1989)
Gould, S.J., *The Mismeasure of Man* (Penguin, 1984)
Grimm, J. & W., *The Complete Grimm's Fairy Tales* (RKP, 1983)
Grojnowski, D., & Sarrazin, B., *L'Esprit fumiste et les rires fin-de-siècle* (Corti, 1990)
Gruzinska, A., 'Octave Mirbeau antimilitariste', *Nineteenth-Century French Studies*, 4 (1975–76), 394–403
—————, 'De la réalité à la fiction: *Le Calvaire* d'Octave Mirbeau', *Les Cahiers naturalistes*, 56 (1982), 131–43
—————, 'Octave Mirbeau's Madame Hanska in "La Mort de Balzac"', *Nineteenth-Century French Studies*, 15 (1986–87), 302–14
Guiral, P., & Thuillier, G., *La Vie quotidienne des domestiques en France au XIXe siècle* (Hachette, 1978)
Gyp, *Le Druide*, 12th edition (Havard, 1885)
Halpern, J., 'Desire and Mask in *Le Journal d'une femme de chambre*', *Kentucky Romance Studies*, 28 (1980), 313–26
Hayman, R., *De Sade: a critical biography* (Constable, 1978)
Herter, K., *Hedgehogs* (Phoenix House, 1965)
Hervieu, P., *Diogène le chien* (Charavay, 1882)
Herzfeld, C., *La Figure de Méduse dans l'œuvre d'Octave Mirbeau* (Nizet, 1992)
Hsü, C.Y.H., *The Rise of Modern China*, 3rd edition (OUP, 1983)

Huret, J., *Enquête sur l'évolution littéraire* (Charpentier, 1891)

James, H., *Daumier Caricaturist* (Rodale Press, 1954)

Jean-Maurienne, *Tribulations de la Société des amis d'Octave Mirbeau* (Société française d'imprimerie et de librairie, 1939)

Jardon, D., *Du comique dans le texte littéraire* (De Boeck-Duculot, 1988)

Kafka, F., *Metamorphosis and Other Stories*, trans. W. & E. Muir (Penguin, 1961)

Kiernan, V.G., *European Empires from Conquest to Collapse, 1815–1960* (Fontana, 1982)

Lacombe, R.G., *Sade et ses masques* (Payot, 1974)

Lamartine, A. de, *Premières méditations*, ed. M. Chervet (Bordas, 1965)

Laux, J.M., *In First Gear: the French automobile industry to 1914* (Liverpool Up, 1976)

Law, G.E., 'Octave Mirbeau and Art: a detailed study of Mirbeau's relationship with artists and an account of his writings on art', Ph.D thesis (University College, London, 1983)

Levin, H., ed., *Veins of Humor* (Cambridge, Mass., Harvard Up, 1972)

Lloyd, C., 'Food and Decadent Culture: J.-K. Huysmans and Octave Mirbeau', *Romance Studies*, 13 (1988), 69–79

——————, *J.-K. Huysmans and the Fin-de-siècle novel* (Edinburgh UP, 1990)

London, J., *The Call of the Wild*, ed. J. Dickey (Penguin, 1981)

Maitron, J., *Le Mouvement anarchiste en France*, vol. 1, *Des origines à 1914* (Maspero, 1983)

Maricourt, T., *Histoire de la littérature libertaire en France* (Albin Michel, 1990)

Martin-Fugier, A., *La Place des bonnes: la domesticité féminine à Paris en 1900* (Grasset, 1979)

Masson, P., *Le Disciple et l'insurgé: roman et politique à la Belle Epoque* (PU de Lyon, 1987)

Michel, P., 'Les «Palinodies» d'Octave Mirbeau: à propos de Mirbeau et de Daudet', *Les Cahiers naturalistes*, 62 (1988), 116–26

——————, 'Mirbeau et l'affaire Gyp', *Littératures*, 26 (1992), 201–19

——————, 'Autour du *Calvaire*: huit lettres d'Octave Mirbeau à Paul Hervieu', idem., 221–56

Michel, P., & Nivet, J.-F., *Octave Mirbeau: l'imprécateur au cœur fidèle* (Séguier, 1990)

Mirbeau, Mme Octave, *La Famille Carmettes* (Charpentier, 1888)

Miroux, A., *Les Défaillances: Jean Marcellin* (Ollendorff, 1885)

Newton, J., 'Emile Zola and Octave Mirbeau: with extracts from their unpublished letters', *Nottingham French Studies*, 25 (1986), 42–59

—————, 'Octave Mirbeau and Auguste Rodin: with extracts from unpublished correspondence', *Laurels*, 58 (1987), 33–60

—————, 'Whistler, Octave Mirbeau and George Moore', *Romance Quarterly*, 37 (1990), 157–63

—————, 'Zola, Mirbeau et les peintres: *L'Œuvret Dans le ciel*', in *Ecrire la peinture*, ed. P. Delaveau (Editions universitaires, 1991) 47–58

Nivet, J.-F., 'Francs-parleurs: Octave Mirbeau et Jules Vallès', *Revue d'études vallésiennes*, 5 (1987), 45–53

—————, 'Mirbeau journaliste', doctoral thesis, 3 vols (Université de Lyon II), 1987

—————, 'Octave Mirbeau entre espoirs et cauchemars', *Les Cahiers naturalistes*, 61 (1987), 218–27

Octave Mirbeau, ed. P. Michel & G. Cesbron (PU d'Angers, 1992)

Overy, R., 'Heralds of Modernity: cars and planes from invention to necessity', in *Fin de Siècle and its Legacy*, ed. M. Teich & R. Porter (CUP, 1990), 54–79)

Palacio, J. de, *Les Perversion du merveilleux: ma Mère l'Oye au tournant du siècle* (Séguier, 1993)

Pilon, E., *Octave Mirbeau* (Bibliothèque internationale d'édition, 1903)

Pugh, S., *Garden—Nature—Language* (Manchester UP, 1988)

Reboux, P., & Müller, C., *A la manière de...* (Grasset, 1913)

Redfern, W.D., 'The Pyromaniac Fireman', *TLS* (14 October 1977), 1197

Regnault, A., *Mademoiselle Pomme*, 2nd edition (Ollendorff, 1886)

Revon, M., *Octave Mirbeau: son œuvre* (Editions de la Nouvelle Revue Critique, 1924)

Rioux, J.-P., *Chronique d'une fin de siècle: France 1889–1900* (Seuil, 1991)

Sade, D.A.F. de, *Œuvres complètes*, vol. 13, *Les 120 Journées de Sodome, ou L'Ecole du libertinage* (Cercle du livre précieux, 1967)

———, *Les Infortunes de la vertu*, intro. by F. Van Laere (Verviers, Marabout, 1975)

———, *La Nouvelle Justine, ou les malheurs de la vertu*, vol. 1, intro. by G. Lely (UGE, 10/18, 1978)

Sapin, L., 'Paris-Madrid automobile', in *La Belle Epoque*, ed. G. Guilleminault (Le Livre de poche, 1966), 145–93

Sarcey, F., *Quarante ans de théâtre*, vol. 7 (Bibliothèque des annales politiques et littéraires, 1901)

Sartre, J.-P., *Qu'est-ce que la littérature?* (Gallimard, Idées, 1978)

Schwarz, M., 'Octave Mirbeau et l'affaire Dreyfus', *French Review*, 39 (1965), 361–72

———, *Octave Mirbeau: vie et œuvre*(The Hague/Paris, Mouton, 1966)

———, 'Une amitié ignorée: Edmond de Goncourt—Octave Mirbeau', *French Review*, 44 (1971), 97–105

Sonn, R.D., *Anarchism and Cultural Politics in Fin-de-siècle France* (University of Nebraska Press, 1989)

Stone, N., *Europe Transformed 1878–1919* (Fontana, 1983)

Storr, A., *Human Aggression* (Penguin, 1970)

Suffel, J., 'Quand Mirbeau faisait scandale', *Journal de Genève* (20–22 May 1961)

Suleiman, S.R., *Authoritarian Fictions: the ideological novel as a literary genre* (New York, Columbia UP, 1983)

Thiéblemont, S., 'Octave Mirbeau: la vie d'un mécène au regard accusateur', doctoral thesis (Université de Nancy II), 1986

Vallès, J., *Œuvres*,vol. 1, ed. R. Bellet (Gallimard, Pléiade, 1975)

Vanseveren, M.-P., & Rombeaut, A., 'La Malle-Poste', *Revue des sciences humaines*, 173 (1979), 137–48

Walker, J.A., 'L'Ironie de la douleur: la vie et la vision d'Octave Mirbeau', Ph.D thesis (University of Toronto, 1954)

Walker, S., *Animal Thought* (RKP, 1983)

Weber, E., *France Fin de Siècle* (Cambridge, Mass., Belknap Press, 1986)

———, 'Speeding into Trouble', *TLS* (23–29 March 1990), 312

Wechsler, J., *A Human Comedy: physiognomy and caricature in nineteenth-century Paris* (Thames & Hudson, 1982)

Woodcock, G., *Anarchism* (Penguin, 1963)

Wright, G., *Between the Guillotine and Liberty: two centuries of the crime problem in France* (OUP, 1983)

Ziegler, R.E., 'Hunting the Peacock: the pursuit of non-reflective experience in Mirbeau's *Le Jardin des supplices*', *Nineteenth-Century French Studies*, 12-13 (1984), 162-74

—————, '«Pour fabriquer un rien»: from education to anarchy in Octave Mirbeau', *Degré second*, 10 (September 1986), 23-30

Note
The illustration on the front cover is taken from the illustration by W.Hyde on the inside cover of a slim volume of poems entitled *The Open Road: A Little Book for Wayfarers* compiled by E.V Lucas (London, Grant Richards, 1899). From a copy in the private collection of Dr. P.G. Starkey.

DURHAM MODERN LANGUAGES SERIES

French

FM1 Richard D. Burton, *The Context of Baudelaire's 'Le Cygne'*. 1980, 102 pp. ISBN 0 907310 01 X. £4.95

FM2 R.J. Howells, *Pierre Jurieu: Antinomian Radical*. 1983, 90 pp. ISBN 0 907310 04 4. £4.95

FT1 Malherbe, Théophile de Viau, and Saint-Amant, *A Selection*. R.G. Maber (ed.), 1983, repr. 1985, 1987; second edition revised, 1991, 132 pp. ISBN 0 907310 08 7. £3.95

FM3 James S. Munro, *Mademoiselle de Scudéry and the 'Carte de Tendre'*. 1986, 97 pp. ISBN 0 907310 12 5. £4.95

FT2 Michel-Jean Sedaine, *Le Philosophe sans le savoir*. Graham E. Rodmell (ed.), 1987, 122 pp. ISBN 0 907310 15 X. £4.95

FM4 David Hillery, *Verlaine: Fixing an Image*. 1988, 105 pp. ISBN 0 907310 18 4. £4.95

FT3 Molière, *Dépit amoureux*. Noël Peacock (ed.), 1990, 150 pp. ISBN 0 907310 20 6. £4.95

FM5 H. Gaston Hall, *Molière's 'Le Bourgeois Gentilhomme': Context and Stagecraft*. 1990, 98 pp. ISBN 0 907310 21 4. £4.95

FM6 Anthony Cheal Pugh (ed.), *France 1940: Literary and Historical Reactions to Defeat*. 1992, 133 pp. ISBN 0 907310 23 0. £6.95

FM7 David Hillery, *Lamartine: The 'Méditations Poétiques'*. 1993, 132 pp. ISBN 1 870530 55 1. £6.95

FM8 Nichola Anne Haxell, *Reflections of the Revolution: Poetry and Prose for the Second French Republic*. 1993, 147 pp. ISBN 0 907310 24 9. £7.95

FT4	La Mothe Le Vayer, *'Lettre sur la Comédie de L'Imposteur'*. Robert Mc Bride (ed.), 1994, 170 pp. ISBN 0 907310 25 7. £8.95
FM9	Christopher Lloyd and Robert Lethbridge (ed.), *Maupassant conteur et romancier*. 1994, 201 pp. ISBN 0 907310 26 5. £9.95
FM10	Richard Maber (ed.), *Nouveaux Mondes: from the Twelfth to the Twentieth Century*. 1994. 149 pp. ISBN 0 907310 27 3. £7.95
FM11	Richard Burton, *Le Flâneur*, 1994. 80pp. ISBN 0907310 28 1. £5.50
FM12	Henry Phillips, *Racine: Language and Theatre*, 1994. 157pp. ISBN 0907310 29 X. £8.95
FM13	Paul Andrew Tipper, *The Dream Machine: Avian Imagery in 'Madame Bovary'*. 1994. 35pp. ISBN 0907310 30 3. £2.95.
FM14	Christopher Lloyd (ed.), *Epidemics and Sickness in French Literature and Culture*. 1995. 199pp. ISBN 0907310 31 1. £8.95.
FM15	Christopher Lloyd, *Mirbeau's Fictions*. 1996. 118pp. ISBN 0 907310 35 4. £8.95.

German

GT1	Hans Sachs, *Selections*. Mary Beare (ed.), 1983, 242 pp. ISBN 0 907310 06 0. £3.50
GM1	Howard Gaskill, *Hölderlin's 'Hyperion'*. 1984, 68 pp. ISBN 0 907310 07 9. £4.95
GM2	Patrick Bridgwater, *The Poet as Hero and Clown: A Study of Heym and Lichtenstein*. 1986, 82 pp. ISBN 0 907310 13 3. £4.95
GM3	Patrick Bridgwater, *George Moore and German Pessimism*. 1988, 81 pp. ISBN 0 907310 17 6. £4.95

GM4	Mark G. Ward, *Laughter, Comedy and Aesthetics: Kleist's 'Der zerbrochne Krug'*. 1989, 87 pp. ISBN 0 907310 22 2. £4.95
GM5	Neil Thomas, *Reading the Nibelungenlied*. 1995, 119 pp. ISBN 0 907310 32 X. £7.95
GM6	Neil Thomas and Françoise Le Saux, *Myth and its Legacy in European Literature*. 1996, 169 pp. ISBN 0 907310 33 8. £8.95

Hispanic

HM1	R.P. Calcraft, *The Sonnets of Luis de Góngora*. 1980, 127 pp. ISBN 0 907310 00 1. £4.95
HM2	Keith Whinnom, *La Poesia amatoria de la época de los Reyes Católicos*. 1981, 112 pp. ISBN 0 907310 02 8. £4.95
HM3	H. Ramsden, *Pío Baroja: 'La busca' 1903 to 'La busca' 1904*. 1982, 90 pp. ISBN 0 907310 05 2. £4.95
HM4	Jack M. Flint, *The Prose Works of Roberto Arlt*. 1985, 96 pp. ISBN 0 907310 09 5. £4.95
HT1	Carlos Fuentes, *Aura*. Peter Standish (ed.), 1986, 53 pp. ISBN 0 907310 10 9. £3.95
HM5	John Crosbie, *A lo divino Lyric Poetry: An Alternative View*. 1989, 92 pp. ISBN 0 907310 19 2. £4.95

Slavonic

SM1	Terence Wade, *Prepositions in Modern Russian*. 1983, repr. 1984, 136 pp. ISBN 0 907310 03 6. £3.95
ST1	V.V. Mayakovsky, *Klop*. Robert Russell (ed.), 1985, 127 pp. ISBN 0 907310 11 7. £3.95
ST2	V.F. Odoyevsky, *Pyostryye skazki*. Neil Cornwell (ed.), 1988, 98 pp. ISBN 0 907310 14 1. £4.95
ST3	Aleksandr Blok, *The Twelve*. Avril Pyman (ed.), 1989, viii + 136 pp. ISBN 0 907310 16 8. £4.95

Further titles in preparation.

All titles may be ordered direct from:

The General Editor,   Tel: 0191 374 2744
Durham Modern Languages Series,   Fax: 0191 374 2716
Elvet Riverside, New Elvet,
Durham DH1 3JT

EU authorised representative for GPSR:
Easy Access System Europe, Mustamäe tee 50,
10621 Tallinn, Estonia
gpsr.requests@easproject.com

www.ingramcontent.com/pod-product-compliance
Ingram Content Group UK Ltd.
Pitfield, Milton Keynes, MK11 3LW, UK
UKHW042121200326
4879IPUK00001B/5